MILLIONAIRE MOM $5K TO $6.5MM REAL ESTATE INVESTING

(You Can, Too!)

A Real-Life Story

Terry Records

Terry Records
Visit my website at www.TerryandJason.com

Printed in the United States of America

First Printing: May 2019

ISBN: 9781091671928

This book is dedicated to my children,
Adam and Nicholas Smith.
We three began this journey together when they were seven
and four years old.
They were my cheerleaders initially, but more importantly,
they were my "Big Why."
A mother will do all she can to provide for a future for her
children.
I wanted them to have every opportunity imaginable.
Thank you for your love, support, eagerness, and openness to
take this journey with me.

Love, Mom

CONTENTS

BEGINNING THE JOURNEY

This book is about my journey
In the beginning, I wasn't even aware I was on a journey
It's interesting how your life is affected by the people who come into your life
They change you
You impact them
This book is my gift to you!
With my Simple Hope
That Something
Big or Small
Make a difference in your life!
I hope to meet you someday!
Hugs!
Terry Records
http://www.TerryandJason.com

PREFACE

THIS BOOK WAS BORN OUT of my own personal journey in generating personal wealth over the course of a decade. That journey started out with a small investment, but through smart choices, I was able to grow $5,000 to $6.5 million in just over 10 years. At the time, few people were doing what I was doing, and there were no models. But my mistakes and challenges are now your benefit, and the possibilities for you are even bigger once you've learned the approach and strategies behind my success. Because I give this material as a seminar and provide real estate investment coaching on the topic, you'll see that we pulled out special sections in each chapter just for you. These FAQs have been taken from real people just like you who have an interest in financial freedom. In almost every case, they were regular people with an interest in wealth generation, not professors talking about theories. And because I've had decades of experience, I'm also offering you insider tips that aren't as well-known. This will help give you an edge when it comes to your own journey toward financial freedom. And while this book tells the story of my own life journey, we've also included an easy-to-use format that allows you to skip around and enjoy the information in the way that makes the most sense to you. Whether you're a novice real estate agent or a seasoned investor, I've included something just for you in this book as I tell my story. And of course, I'm always available via email to answer your questions and provide one-on-one coaching opportunities.

CHAPTER 1

YOUR PATH TO WEALTH STARTS WITH A PRINCIPAL RESIDENCE

This chapter begins our journey into the world of personal wealth creation. It's also the first step in my own personal story of how I learned to generate stable investment income and gain financial independence at the same time. And if you don't yet own a principal residence, don't worry, because we're going to see how that can work to your advantage too.

In this chapter, you'll learn about:

- The importance of choosing a principal residence
- Buying strategically from the beginning
- The power of independent thinking
- Recognizing a diamond in the rough

Take a moment and imagine it for yourself: Summit Avenue in St. Paul, Minnesota. Along the road in front of a number of brownstone row houses and large extraordinary Victorian homes, snow continues to pile up and a tour bus passes by. Just next door, F. Scott Fitzgerald once spent his days, writing his famous debut novel *This Side of Paradise*. Even then, the properties on this street were known for their somewhat controversial architecture.

And as tourists in 1991 snapped photos, you could understand why the homes still had their reputation. With a distinctive look, each row house is set in its own take on Victorian style, but with each one differing from the others. They were typical for the part of town they were in, and at the time, 599 Summit Avenue, or the F. Scott Fitzgerald House, was already on the National Historic Landmark list. While it alone attracted its fair share of sightseers, this particular row house, adjacent to the F. Scott Fitzgerald home, was not one that most real estate agents or investors were considering, not for investment potential. Even though it had an abundance of space, it was tired and ugly with major problems lurking in every corner.

Except one person was taking note of the possibilities. Back then, as a rookie real estate agent, I was still learning all the ins and outs of buying and selling properties. I was also recently divorced, had two little boys in tow with me, and had yet to learn just how important the decision I was about to make would be. And long before I had made my first million dollars or attained the financial freedom I value so much today, I also simply needed somewhere to live.

As luck would have it, there was property available to purchase on Summit Avenue. In fact, there was 4,000 sq. ft of property, complete with 1960s paneling throughout but zero walls underneath, floors which looked like they had been through a war-zone, curtain-less windows, a leaking roof and a whole host of other less than desirable aspects. At the time, it was a property in an area just about no one was taking interest in, outside of those tourists who occasionally gawked at the architectural details.

But if you can picture it with me for a moment, the staircase that spiraled up, while in desperate need of work, had its own subtle, majestic charm. The dilapidated, empty spots in a few areas were begging for historic lighting to elevate this space. The hardwood floors were just waiting to be completely redone. And under that paneling? There were electrical extension cords underneath for "wiring." And well... I wasn't sure what I was going to do about those, not yet anyway. Still, my boys and I needed a place to live, and through what was essentially seller financing, I put down a small down payment, and I purchased all 4,000 sq. ft, blemishes and all. Yet, I had no way of knowing that this small decision of buying a less-than-ideal property would launch my journey to becoming a multi-millionaire in just over a decade.

For the first two years, I did nothing but eat, work, and sleep in the home. Luckily, the seller had agreed to carry that contract for deed through to three years while I worked on the property. But as you can imagine, between building a career as a real estate agent and being a mother, I had a lot going on. At the same time, improving upon the property was at the forefront of my mind. Of course, what my boys, Adam and Nick, remember most are the bats.

Yes, the bats. Looking back on my path to wealth generation, that beginning was actually quite funny. At first, we thought it was just the three of us living in this huge brownstone, at least until I started hearing squeaks inside my bedroom walls. The sounds kept coming closer and closer, and I got scared. I even slept with the light on a couple nights until, all the sudden, I awoke and saw three creatures flying beside the ceiling fan above my bed. I shrieked and ran for protection, right into the kids' bedroom, and I immediately slammed the door like they would protect me!

Long story short: we spent some time trying to get rid of those bats and even called someone to come rescue us but to no avail. We never did find them again, at least not all of them. The next morning, I was bathing in my luscious clawfoot bathtub, a style of bathtub that I love. Nearby, the boys were brushing their teeth at the sink.

"Mom, remember those bats?" Adam said. "Well, I found one. It's hanging on the soap dish beside you in the tub!"

You might not have imagined a story about financial freedom starting out with bats. However, as we'll see, the journey to financial freedom can begin almost anywhere. This is especially true if you haven't purchased your first property, because you can maximize those early decision on your path to wealth.

Of course, for my story, I didn't have the money to rehab my property just yet. During those three years, I was busy working hard each day at my job, creating money to live on, and hopefully, earning enough extra cash to fix the home in the near future. My philosophy was, even if I never could earn enough money to fix it, I knew I was still "money-ahead" by not paying rent. I decided merely living in a strategically purchased home, one I believed would appreciate by at least the amount of my monthly mortgage payment, would be a good investment. Bottom-line: I ultimately would be living for free.

And today? Properties on that same street are worth half a million dollars or more. Some are worth millions.

Now, before you read on, spend a minute or two considering how a strategic purchase like that one could put *you* on the road to financial freedom. If you could buy a property or asset for pennies on the dollar and years before anyone else bothered to look at it, would you be able to recognize its value? You probably don't have a difficult time recognizing the importance of increased value over time, but there's even more to the story, much more.

About 18 months later, after I completed by first rental project, I had a little cash and was able to completely transform it. From a principal residence few would want at the time to a desirable and attractive home to live in, it would eventually undergo a renovation. And that's just the start. From redoing all the walling and sanding the floors to upgrading the lighting and enhancing the entire space, I strategically chose renovation projects to maximize the future dollar potential, whether I would choose to live in it forever, rent it, or just sell it outright. I didn't add the new kitchen, baths, or a garage (yep, no parking here). At the time, they weren't in my budget. And really, I could get more bang out of my buck by doing renovations such as painting, sanding, and pre-habbing the home, getting rid of unnecessary paneling and clutter.

By doing so, the original charm of the home began to show. Of course, I simply was doing the most I could with what I had at the time and saved expensive items for the future owner to complete. By getting the home clean, open, and neat for the future home-owner, I was preparing it, so they could create a vision for their new home. You might be thinking how, by pre-habbing the home, I left money on the table for the next owner, but in reality, I also made plenty for myself. At the same time, I also capitalized on important tax-savings the government allows by selling your principal residence according to the IRS standards.

And because I had identified its potential value beforehand, I was able to use it as my first stepping stone in a journey to complete financial freedom. First and foremost, I obviously had to live

3

somewhere. But by finding a "diamond in the rough," I was able to greatly leverage the possibilities that lay ahead of me, as we'll soon see. The bottom-line, however, is that you want to choose your principal residence carefully for several reasons.

First, in most cases, this initial investment can be done with very little down, especially when you look at those "diamonds in the rough." Believe it or not, there are numerous such properties across the country. At the time of my purchase, I didn't have to put much money down on my Summit Avenue property. Additionally, and of equal importance, it's a fact that the majority of people will at some point buy a home to live in. By positioning themselves to jump from renting to owning, and doing it intelligently, they can open a world of options, options closed off for them before. At the same time, they're taking their first steps to wealth creation.

Second, taxes. There's always taxes, right? We'll talk about taxes again later in the book, but on your road to financial freedom, the time you'll likely enjoy lower taxes without difficulty is when you purchase your principal residence. And because it represents the beginning of your journey, taking advantage of those lower taxes can be a big help for many of us. You see, our current tax system treats homeowners favorably if they've lived in their principal residence two of the last five years. In fact, a single person with gains of $250,000 on their principal residence can sell it and pay NO tax. Hard to believe, right? Just be sure to always check with your tax professional.

Really, everyone should be playing the principal residence game; it's that important.

Why don't more people play it then? One reason: the danger of loving your home too much and then you won't be open to selling it. This is just one of the many tips we're going to learn about throughout our journey together. As we'll also see, financial freedom isn't about starting out filthy rich. In fact, the very opposite can be true: it's about setting goals and taking small steps in the right direction... at all times.

Third and finally for this chapter, easy upgrades to a well-chosen property needing a little love can go a long, long way. Just think about your own current residence. What could be done to enhance the property, and in turn, raise the rents if it's a rental property, for example? When you strategically choose a property to improve and one that's situated in an area that is transitional and likely to get increased attention as a neighborhood, you're setting the stage for a double bump in appreciation. The home will improve with your repairs, but also increase in value when the neighborhood transitions. In the case of my investing career, we'll see how neighborhoods change over time. If you choose one that is deteriorating, for example, your value will go down, and the converse is true. And this is why it's important to consult with a professional when making decisions. For me, I've seen a majority of homeowners over-improving their homes because of a personal "want or desire." If you want to build wealth, you want to be "objective" instead of "subjective," making the right decisions to lead to outcomes that meet your goals.

As we'll also find out in future chapters, you can't merely follow the crowd in finding these market anomalies. But when you spend that little bit of extra time hunting one down and accepting it as it is for the time being, you're paving the way for your own financial success in a way that can be truly incredible.

This is our first step together on the road to wealth generation. As you can see, my story to financial freedom starts in the most unlikely of places. But no matter where you're starting, armed with this book and the decades of experience in it, you'll be off to a good start.

Frequently Asked Questions

Q: How do you identify properties with strategic value when choosing your first principal residence?

A: Choosing any property is a balance of many factors, and as we'll see throughout this book, every investment situation is different. However, we'll pick up a number of principles in coming chapters to help you identify strategic value in any avenue of your life. The most important thing to consider is: What's your goal? What are you trying to accomplish? One strategy might be right for one person, but not for another.

Q: How important was it for you to be a real estate agent when you started your journey?

A: Although I valued my experience as a real estate agent, I was still a rookie when I bought my principal residence. In reality, recognizing future possibilities was far more instrumental in my decision, and you definitely don't have to be an expert in real estate to practice that skill. It's actually more helpful if you find a very experienced individual to be part of your team of professionals to guide you.

And not all real estate agents are created equal either. Perhaps less than 1% of them who I've encountered can teach you the principles I'm going to teach you in this book and subsequent book titled *Should You Rent it? Flip it? or Run?* It's critical that you interview many real estate agents when you decide to work with one. Take a recent example I came across: I encountered a new client who proudly told me that they had just bought five properties to flip. I cringed inside knowing it was not possible in our current market.

I set up a time to view the properties, and the client was disappointed when I told them they had actually purchased five rental properties, not flips. You see, the agent they used... she heard the client tell her that they wanted to fix-up properties and re-sell. So, she found projects, just not property that allowed them to meet their fix-up goals, a crucial but common mistake. This mistake caused the investor to abandon his previous goal of being a full-time investor and take another "job" working for someone else. They could have been enjoying financial freedom instead if they had read this book!

Q: How do you avoid buying during a bubble or how do you time the market when purchasing your principal residence?

A: Understanding Market Timing is key to building wealth with real estate. When it comes down to it, different techniques work at different times in each individual marketplace. We'll be discussing Market Timing in depth, so hold onto this question as we move forward. As we'll see toward the end of our journey, financial freedom is less about perfect timing and more about recognizing the signs of broader cycles throughout the economy and understanding your own financial situation. If you always own a principal residence, it really doesn't matter as much about timing though. If you can sell at the high point of the market and replace with a new project principal residence, you're most assured to win.

Insider's Tip

For many people, becoming attached to their principal residence can be very tempting. And when you think about it, it makes perfect sense. Your principal residence becomes your home, but there's a bigger picture at stake. For every renovation project you do, first crunch the numbers with a seasoned professional. This way, you'll ensure that you're objectively adding to the potential value of your property, rather than merely upgrading at random or by what you like best. Think about buying your principal residence as a stepping stone and each time when it's time to sell it, you're one step closer to achieving your dream of financial freedom.

Investor Bonus

You're probably already wondering how you'll juggle all the demands involved with being a successful investor. As you can see, because of how my journey to wealth creation started, I can appreciate the importance of prioritizing your time.

With that in mind, I want to offer you an investor bonus to aid in your journey. Now that you have my book in your hand, head over to my site to get your *free* audio copy of this book, so you can have both resources at your fingertips. Use this link to get your *free* copy now:

http://terryandjason.pages.ontraport.net/free5kto6.5million

CHAPTER 2

TAKE STOCK OF YOUR RESOURCES & YOUR FINANCES

This chapter provides you with a jumping off point to fully understand how you can secure your principal residence, but also, where you can start if you have other assets. We'll review why it's so vital to take stock of your resources and how you can do so in a smart, organized way.

In this chapter, you'll learn about:

- The need to take an assessment of your current financial position
- Using all the financial resources at your disposal
- The future possibilities your lifestyle can open up for you
- Your planning options and how they can guide you through the process

So, you know you want financial freedom, but how do you know where to start once you've decided that you want it? This question is a frequent one during my seminars on wealth creation. In fact, I regularly meet people who are eager to attain financial freedom but aren't exactly sure where to start. Many of them dream about having their own business, while others consider playing the stock market. Some of them have put away a small nest egg to jump-start their journey, and still others want to escape their current employment situation and live on their own terms.

Whatever your reason for desiring financial freedom and whatever your unique situation is, you must start by taking stock of your resources. Even if you feel like you have little to work with, you need to have the specifics laid out in front of you, so you know which opportunities make the most sense for you at this point in time. After all, if you're not sure what your current financial situation is, how will you make the step to a better one?

Now, before we dive into organizing and taking stock of your situation, I want to reiterate a point from our first chapter. It's a point we'll see reiterated later in our journey, but it's especially important right now as well. What could have possibly been so vital to my first steps in attaining millions of dollars?

When it comes down to it, you may feel like you're limited in your financial resources. I've spoken with countless people over the years who have felt this way, even ones who had saved considerable sums or had access to substantial equity. It can be very tempting when you start your own journey into financial freedom to think you don't need to take stock of your resources due to this feeling. Yet, nothing could be further from the truth.

You'll remember from our previous chapter that when I started my own journey, I was merely a rookie real estate agent. Not only did I not have access to a huge checkbook, I also had two little boys who I had to care and provide a life for. By organizing myself and taking stock of my resources, I knew that I would be able to make the smartest decisions about the opportunities available to me at that moment in time. Most importantly, I knew that any risks I would need to make would be carefully chosen to leverage the rewards but also, any possible pitfalls.

By now, you're probably starting to see that financial freedom and wealth creation aren't about gambling. Sure, there's risk involved but not the blind risk of a roulette table. Instead, when you list out all the resources at your disposal, you're able to use each and every one of them in clearly defined ways to obtain your goals. It can mean the difference between losing your starting investments or launching yourself into financial freedom.

So, how do you get started, and what sorts of guides are available to make this task easier for you? Unlike when I started my journey, you can find a number of financial checklists and audit sheets available online. However, now that you know how important this step is, see my Insider's Tip at the end of this chapter for an excellent resource to take stock of your financial resources.

But to hit this point home, let's compare two situations. In the first, a cash-strapped single mother with a career inherits $5,000. She's kept her credit score at a respectable level, worked hard, and bought a generously sized principal residence that needs rehab. While her resources were modest, by taking stock of them, she was able to see where her opportunities were, seize them, and take the next step of buying her first rental property with that $5,000 inheritance. And then she began generating additional cash flow.

Our second example is a bit different. In fact, you may even have read or heard about similar situations. In this scenario, a young man hits it big in the music world and is suddenly flush with money. Let's say that it's a lot of money, in the millions, and there's more offers coming in. Instead of taking stock of his financial resources and making sound decisions, the young man goes on a spending spree. We all probably know how this story ends... a few years later, the young man not only isn't generating wealth anymore, he's millions of dollars in debt. How can this situation happen?

Without doing a thorough review of your financial situation, you won't just miss the opportunities to generate more wealth. In many cases, because you aren't truly aware of your finances, you're likely to live beyond your means and slip further into debt, no matter how much money you start out with.

Doing a sound financial audit of your current situation doesn't have to be overly complicated either. Through the work involved, you'll see what options are available to you right now, not five years from now or ten years from now. *Right now.* And finally, when you have that perspective, you can make the necessary decisions in your lifestyle to set yourself up for future rewards and secure your long-term freedom and desires.

Do you have a job? Do you need a job? Can you qualify for loans? What is your credit score? Does it matter? How much cash do you have? Can you access any other cash? Can you leverage property? Do you have access to other people's money? Self-directed IRAs? Home-equity lines of credit? Private lenders? Reverse mortgage opportunities? These questions are only the start. But you'll want to sit down with a professional and evaluate your situation. In doing so, you should be able to identify the first one to three next steps you need to take on the way to financial freedom and wealth building. It's not important to know everything at once but to know the right path and begin your journey.

Frequently Asked Questions

Q: What if you don't yet have a principal residence of your own?
A: That's perfect! Your first best choice in buying and building wealth should be your principal residence. We always start with evaluating the principal residence component, and then we create an investment strategy that meets each individual's personal goals.

Q: What did people say to you when you first started your journey to financial freedom?
A: They thought that I was crazy as I looked at properties in areas they would never consider and as I talked about the potential these homes had. Today, when I look back at the wealth I've generated, I know it's not always smart to follow the wisdom of the crowd. As we'll see later in the book when we talk about connecting the dots, and even later, when we talk about the financial crash of 2008, that desire to think for oneself is the bedrock of wealth creation.

Q: What is the single most important thing to consider when building wealth?

A: The most important thing you can do is to sit down and set your own long-term and short-term goals. And I don't just mean with regards to real estate. Think long and hard. What do you want to be doing in three to five years? Who do you want in your life? What does that picture look like? How does it feel? Dive deep until you have a clear vision of your future. I spend months visualizing my long-term goals. As Jim Rohn said, "Everyone can completely change the direction of their life every three to five years." You just have to decide you want to change. Unless you create your goals and a vision of what those goals look like, you won't take the necessary steps to achieve them. You'll be doing the same thing three to five years from now and won't be able to act on opportunity that comes your way in the meantime.

Insider's Tip

Some of the biggest questions you can ask yourself during this part of your journey are very simple and yet so insightful. What are you willing to sacrifice in order to obtain your goals? What are you willing to give up? What steps do you need to take? What obstacles are in your way?

CHAPTER 3

GOAL PLANNING BY ACCIDENT & MY FIRST INVESTMENT PURCHASE

This chapter truly showcases how there's growth potential for just about every unique financial situation out there. You'll learn how recognizing opportunities in the moment can lead to larger strategies and how these strategies can serve you well over the years. You'll also see why no one can necessarily teach you one secret to wealth creation that works every single time.

In this chapter, you'll learn about:
- Feeding smaller goals into your larger vision
- Flexibility as a vital skill for wealth creation
- How financial surprises come in the most unlikely places
- Your first steps in understanding Market Timing

T he next step in my personal story of wealth creation was almost completely by accident. If I had been content to merely renovate my row house on Summit Avenue, our journey would likely be at an end. In fact, I might not have gone on to invest in countless other properties, start businesses, nor hold millions of dollars in assets. So, what happened?

My smaller goal of needing a cost-effective place to live was accomplished. Plus, the row house on Summit Avenue was comfortable and livable, and life wasn't too bad. Sure, the market was still a bit sluggish, but that wasn't anything completely out of the ordinary.

Then one weekend came that would change everything.

In working the "job," as they say, part of being a real estate agent, I held an open house all day on Saturday and Sunday. This was at the request of the bank that owned two of my listings at the time. And the bank had the idea that if I held an open house on their two row houses at 230 and 232

N. Dale Street in St. Paul all weekend, a flood of offers would fall into place if they had me market them as a "sealed bid" offer.

Well, I stood there *all* weekend. One side of the properties was condemned, but it had heat. Did I mention... it was the middle of winter? And, the other side—well, it had no heat. Did I also mention that Dale Street is an EXTREMELY BUSY street and that there was an abundance of crime in the area at the time?

And as I spent my entire weekend in those foreclosed units, I had time to think. Of course, it didn't take long before I started to imagine what I could do with them. What possibilities did I imagine? For starters, I had these units listed for $12,900 each, and they had been on the market over 200 days. No one wanted them, and I mean no one.

As I thought, I suddenly realized that my Grandpa Aiken had just left me $5,000 at his passing. And at some point, I wondered if I really should buy these properties. What were the possibilities, and what could I do with them? That's when I decided that I wanted them, and I would offer the bank $5,011 each, utilizing my inheritance and a credit card to purchase them. Sounds a little out-of-the-ordinary, doesn't it?

On Monday, I submitted my two "sealed offers." And as it turns out, mine were not the only offers on the table. However, while the others were for $7,500 each, the bank chose mine. As it turns out, the other buyer had previously offered $12,900 and backed out. So, the bank took my offer, and let me apply my $1,000 commission to each side, allowing me to make the purchase for $4,011 each!

But now what?

You would think that the other agents in my office would have been jealous. But no, that wasn't the case. The old-timer agents just snickered at me to my face and said, "What the hell are you doing? Rentals in *that* area? blah..."

But now the work really started. I needed a handyman, painter, carpet installer, and plumber. And that was just the start. Truthfully, with everything involved, I didn't know where to begin. Yet, I had to start somewhere. So, I began with personal referrals and then tried a few local experts. As it turns out, a few were homeruns, while others took advantage of me. How did I handle it all? I quickly identified problems, modified immediately, and fired on-the-spot when necessary to get the work done.

After a few months of challenging work, the two units were finally ready for tenants. And near the end of the rehab, I started advertising for tenants. Of course, this being my first investment property, I didn't really know what I was doing, and the "old-time" agents in my office weren't giving me any pointers. In the end, I would rent to single women with children on Section 8. And they were happy in their newly renovated three-bedroom one-bath homes paying $650 rent! At the same time, I was happy too. Now I had someone else paying me money that contributed to my cash flow per month.

You see, between renovations and credit cards, my cash was tied up. The worst part was that most banks were pretty hesitant during this period to give out loans. During this time, we were in a part of the market cycle known as "early absorption." This term is our first, but not last, technical financial term. If complex investment analysis and fancy terms aren't usually your thing, don't worry. This concept is fairly straightforward, and for right now, all you need to know is, during this type of market phase, there's not a lot of credit going around. Lenders are worried about loaning money and getting it paid back, and most times, the broader market isn't so hot. Back then, no one was really teaching this concept, but I later learned that it's one of the most important concepts to grasp in the real estate business.

Back to our story: so, banks were hesitant to give out loans, but I was already starting to look for ways to get my cash back. Now, sure, I was able to rent out the units over time, and this freed up a little cash flow, but only a modest amount. And when you're doing all those renovations and paying for general upkeep, cash can be tight.

So, I went to Norwest Mortgage. Even though we were in a period of early market absorption, and the banks were not dishing out many loans, I knew that I had to try. Well, even with the current market conditions, I was able to convince them to appraise the Dale Street properties. Now, it wasn't easy by any means. In fact, I had to show them all my taxes going back years and all my earnings. It felt like they were making me account for every single dime I had earned or held.

Each property would appraise for $40,000 nearly 18 months later. And from there, I was able to place a $25,000 loan on each property and take my $50,000. What did I do with the money? First, I paid off my credit cards, and then I began thinking about buying another property. I also would use some of the cash to fix-up my principal residence on Summit Avenue, which had been patiently waiting major repairs.

And the magic of this situation is this: I was able to get ALL my cash PLUS more cash out to improve my residence and buy another property to rehab. I also created more cash flow, all while KEEPING an asset that still provided a net monthly cash flow of $664.

I was giddy. You can only imagine how I felt, but here I was, still in the 1990s, and still fairly green in my career as a real estate agent, during a challenging time in the market, and the bank was telling me my property was worth $80,000. Imagine if I had never bothered with those units! Or what if I had never bothered to fix them up? And an even bigger question I was asking myself was what if I had skipped going to Norwest Mortgage that day?

And I loved that those "old-timers" in my office still had their noses in the air. It was like they were watching from the sidelines and hoping the new "Rookie of the Year," an official title I would earn for all my efforts, would fail. All they wanted to tell me was "I told you so" when I lost my investment. But I continued, motivated by my own personal goals despite them.

To start, my original goal was for my car payment to be covered by passive income from a rental property. And I had achieved that goal. On the one hand, it took me nearly 18 months, because I didn't have a model to follow or a coach to give me any direction. Anyone can achieve goals like these in a much shorter time period if they find the right coach and model to follow.

And that got me thinking. What if these little goals lead to bigger goals, and from there, even bigger ones? I didn't know it yet, but I was on the path to financial freedom. By taking stock of what resources I had, I was able to start hitting my little financial goals. And it felt really, *really* good!

So, I started to dream a bit bigger.

Soon, and I half-wondered if I could create enough cash flow per month to pay my entire house payment. I felt at the time that this was a HUGE DREAM to me. No one I knew was doing anything of the sort back then. Now, remember, this was during a period of "early absorption" in the market, when credit was scarce and "cash was king," as they say. Using the one to generate the other wasn't exactly being taught at your local schools. Yet, almost by accident, I had learned the strategic value of financial planning and goal setting. Not only that, but I learned how incredibly liberating it was.

Instead of becoming tied to my Dale Street properties, I stayed flexible and kept my eye on the bigger picture. Still, I also kept my goals, however small at the time, in my sights. By doing so, I was able to make my first car payment through wealth generation and get a glimpse at even bigger possibilities. As we'll soon see, these future possibilities were astonishingly large, though I didn't exactly know that fact just yet nor had I learned to dream big enough.

Frequently Asked Questions

Q: If flexibility is key, how do you also strategically plan?
A: This question is an excellent one and often asked in my seminars on wealth creation. Many people assume that flexibility is like making decisions spontaneously and is opposed to methodical planning. Yet, nothing could be further from the truth. Planning to be flexible is itself a strategy for dealing with what life (and your financial situation) brings you. This way, you can make the most out of it. If you know what your goals are, you'll recognize opportunity and be able to take action. Life will present you with many opportunities, and it's up to you which opportunity you seize as you take educated risks.

Q: How do you maintain your perspective during surprising or even challenging times?
A: In the beginning, everything is new to you. Every decision and every problem will take lots of energy and time to solve because you're learning. Fortunately, 95% of the learning is a finite amount

of learning. Once you have the answer to a set of problems, you already have the answer for next time. So, you'll solve that problem the second time without another thought. But when you're faced with a financial surprise or a serious challenge, be open. Consult with someone who knows the answer and can help you minimize the stress. Others have done this before you, just ask. On that note, you always have a resource for one-on-one investment coaching right at your fingertips. Get answers to your most pressing investment questions from someone who's been there. Simply head over to my site to book an individual session now with this link:

http://www.TerryandJason.com/Apply

Q: Can I dream or plan too big?

A: Never. If anything, my biggest mistake and one you can learn from right now, is that I could have dreamt bigger right from the start. Sure, you want to be realistic with your timeframe, but my advice is always this: be ready to dream bigger. The dream must be big enough.

Insider's Tip

Although your vision may change over the years, having one is critical. Whether you want to pay your car payment through rental income or you want to one day own a stunning sailboat you use every single day, the fact remains the same. Your vision is what will help guide you, motivate you, and keep you going even in the face of naysayers.

CHAPTER 4

EVALUATING YOUR MARKETPLACE

In "Evaluating Your Marketplace," you'll discover how markets, from real estate to cryptocurrency, undergo cycles that can last for decades or even longer. You'll also learn how merely hearing about an opportunity in the news likely means that opportunity may have passed and how critical it is for you to connect the dots on your own.

In this chapter, you'll learn about:

- Anticipating "momentum" and market trends
- Focusing on your cash liquidity
- Avoiding the wisdom of the crowd
- Conducting your own research
- Basic trends regarding Market Timing

I f you're reading it in the newspaper... you're too late. The same advice applies as much to the traditional newspapers as it does to major online investing websites. The fact of the matter is, by the time an opportunity has hit the news, you've lost a vital edge that can mean the difference between wealth creation or "sunk costs."

Don't let this next financial term, "sunk costs," scare you off. We'll be going through a few terms in this chapter, but each will be related back in an easy-to-understand way. Best of all, every term we discuss will be tied into my real-world experiences as an investor, not simply some abstract, difficult textbook definition. This way, whether you've made a few investments yourself or you're just starting your steps into the marketplace, you'll be able to draw valuable lessons from my financial journey.

Now, let's dive back in.

If you're reading it in the newspaper... it's almost certainly too late. When you read this statement, you might hesitate for a moment. Especially in situations like the stock market rally preceding the 2008 financial crash, everyone seems to say that there's no end in sight during these moments. You'll even hear people, friends and family perhaps, tell you the good times will go on forever. And after all, didn't plenty of financial trends continue for many years after first being reported in the news?

Of course, the answer is "yes," but the situation isn't as straightforward as you might imagine. And time and time again, my experience has confirmed a number of fundamental principles regarding how markets work. We'll look at several of these in more detail now.

You probably don't have to guess that human psychology plays a role in our story. Just about everyone has heard stories of how an investor let emotion get the best of them, and these investors suffered the consequences. Sometimes the consequences were even in the billions of dollars.

So, what went wrong? Over the years, I've seen countless people enter an opportunity when they read about it in the news. I'll even admit that the temptation was strong for me to do so when I first started my journey into financial freedom. Remember when people were calling me crazy for buying property on Dale Street? It's difficult in a situation like that one not to at least ask yourself whether it's the right thing to do at the time or whether the investment you're hearing everyone talk about is better.

In reality, by the time you've heard about it in the news, smart investors have started to get out of that opportunity. In the investing world, they even have a saying for it now: "buy the rumor; sell the news." What this means is that savvy investors, experienced ones, don't let the emotion of hearing about an opportunity from others influence their decisions. I certainly didn't when I bought my Dale Street properties ahead of other investors. Yet, investors also recognize that they can maximize their potential wealth by leveraging those same human emotions that people possess to naturally follow the crowd.

Though the term wasn't well-known when I began my journey, "sunk costs" was a very real experience for many investors by then and since the founding of the stock market. "Sunk costs," in its most basic form, is the very human emotion to hold a losing position even after serious losses begin, hoping for a change in circumstances. This emotion is commonplace and completely natural. Now that you know about it, you'll see it everywhere from the gambling table to your workplace.

And do you know who is most likely to give into it and hold an investment even after the market has turned? Investors who have followed the crowd blindly into an opportunity after that trend has already developed. Now, there's nothing special about being new to the investing game, making someone more vulnerable to this issue. In fact, there's a possibility that some people give into it more readily than others.

So, what's going on? Think back to my purchase of the Dale Street property. Instead of listening to the experts, the newspapers, or even my friends, I asked myself a number of questions. That's it! And at the same time, they weren't even complex questions; just questions about what I myself saw happening around me. For me, it was important to get the data, take the time, and learn for myself what opportunities were available at what potential future reward.

When you think about it, shouldn't a savvy investor know their market better than even the newspapers? If you know your marketplace, truly know it, you can sell that property you may have bought, that "diamond in the rough," well in advance of the crowd's peak. In fact, you can work with the market's "momentum," how fast the price is going in either direction, because in reality, you're the one getting to opportunities first, instead of entering during the risky phase of a bubble. Like a coach commanding your team, you don't need to rely on a journalist to get the news, because you're the one making it.

Let's take this idea a step further.

By being that savvy investor, that person asking questions and seeking out the data, that person who's thinking for themselves, you're able to begin mastering your emotions. At the same time, you'll be able to formulate multiple exit strategies for your given financial landscape. And remember: everyone's situation is unique, so you're definitely not going to read about multiple exit plans that apply directly to you in the newspapers or investing websites.

The end result is that you're not at the whim of the market cycles, those long trends of boom and bust in every market, from real estate to stock trading. Sure, even with your finger on the pulse of your marketplace, you'll need to "take what the market gives you," as they say; meaning, you'll follow those opportunities that exist currently. Yet, you're no longer at the mercy of the crowds who are jumping to gamble away their money instead of making intelligent, calculated financial decisions. That's exactly what I did when I bought my Dale Street properties, seeing an opportunity in a down market that was on the cusp of shifting directions.

For many people, this philosophy is a dramatic shift in thinking. When you realize that investors know the crowd is irrational, and these investors not only avoid it, some take advantage of it, you can start to see why it's so critical to be on top of the data and information yourself.

And really, it doesn't require any special skill, just your own intuition and the ability to follow what interests you most in your marketplace. No need to know fancy terms like "credit default swaps," "MOB spreads," or any others. Of course, not if you don't have an interest in them and not if they don't apply to your specific investments.

Just like when I saw that attaining the cash flow from my Dale Street properties changed the game for me, you only need to be armed with your own intelligence to spot an opportunity before others do. In coming chapters, we'll look at specific ways to find them on your own. However, for now, skip the newspapers, and get your hands-on charts, spreadsheets, and calendars.

Frequently Asked Questions

Q: What are the most important factors to watch for in market cycles?

A: I love to get this question in my seminars on financial freedom. And the answer is simple: the direction of the crowd, the momentum of price trends, and the creation of market anomalies. Now that we've touched a bit on the "wisdom of the crowd," we'll return to the other two factors later in the chapters devoted to them.

Q: How do you anticipate market trends before they happen?

A: By developing a passion for your marketplace, a passion transcending mere "shop talk" and verging on an obsession. At the same time, that obsession doesn't have to consume your life. In actuality, the opposite is true: you'll be able to get ahead of the crowd and secure financial freedom for your life.

Q: What factors are most critical in knowing when markets are starting to shift?

A: While perfect Market Timing isn't possible, you can definitely get a sense of where things are headed when you're tapped into your market. And the key is to know yours intensely. When you do, you'll begin to notice when factors change slightly. Take note when there's a trend of homes taking longer to sell. For example, when the local board of real estate agents shows statistics of trends over three to six months, perhaps you notice extra inventory staying on the market, taking homes longer to sell. This piece of data can be a sign the market is changing from a seller's market to a buyer's market. Don't get me wrong, homes sell during all phases of the market. But the important thing to consider is your goal with a property. Depending on the phase we're in, different strategies are more effective. In a later chapter, we'll address these techniques in more detail.

Insider's Tip

Keep an active network of disparate professionals, from construction works to financial managers, to give you a solid heads up on breaking news as it hits the wire. Be interested in the broader picture but also the details.

You can also pick up an excellent, *free* resource on Market Timing right from my website. Just use this link to download your copy now:

http://www.TerryandJason.com/Downloads

CHAPTER 5

MY EARLY LESSONS

This chapter describes my first intentional investment purchase. While I had made other strategic wealth decisions leading up to this one, this investment represented the step toward accelerating my plan and bringing it to fruition.

In this chapter, you'll learn about:
- Deploying your financial resources
- Understanding how to take risks
- Recognizing solid investments in the moment
- Putting together a reliable list of partners

Returning to St. Paul, Minnesota and our story, let's ask ourselves: had I attained financial freedom yet? For many people, this chapter would be the end of the road, and the answer would be "yes!" Ultimately, purchasing a property for pennies on the dollar, polishing it up, and having its value increase does sound pretty good, right?

Well, hold on just a moment. Why should I have stopped there? Sure, I could have been content with where I was, but there's far more to the story than just buying distressed property and fixing it up. Truthfully, the possibilities are much, much bigger than just this simple start. Although I had done well, and I felt vindicated in my initial choices, I started thinking.

What if there was more? What if I could pay my house payment each month?

And there it was: the spark of financial freedom.

With a mere $5,000 inheritance and a credit card, and by connecting the dots on my own, I was able to invest in turning some of those same row houses on Dale Street into rental properties. Even though one of them was condemned and didn't even have heat, I soon had an entire team of plumbers, electricians, painters, and more working on them. From interviewing the first contractor to realizing I would have to find my first tenants, I knew I was on the path to something different.

Of course, when I started discussing renting out these properties, from the very start, the old school real estate agents in my office repeatedly told me I was crazy. For them, real estate had a very specific definition and method, and what I was doing certainly didn't look like what they were expecting. Why would anyone rent these properties in what was still a less than desirable neighborhood?

But again, against all the "advice" of naysayers, I put out my first ad. From there, the tenants started calling.

At the time, I was surprised to have them ask about Section 8. This was way before the term was in widespread use, and I had no idea such a program even existed. I was soon to find out how, by allowing Section 8 for my properties, I was providing much-needed housing to people like other single mothers.

Sure, once in a while that meant someone left a couch in the alleyway. Yet, that challenge, and it wasn't a huge one by any means, didn't stop me. For me, it was simply a matter of paying someone to remove the couch. Crazy idea, right? It's only irritating if you allow it to be.

The bottom-line was that I was now deploying my financial resources to take advantage of an opportunity I had seen, one few others were taking advantage of. And in the process, I was helping people, which felt pretty amazing as well. So, how did I know that this risk was worth taking, and how did I recognize this investment in the moment?

Over the next couple years, gentrification began its slow creep toward Dale Street. While it would still be some time before it arrived, I saw how rents were raising. First, they went from low pricing to just a small bump. When a tenant gave notice, I also witnessed a large volume of interest. And by now, I was watching rents in town. So, I decided to raise my rents to $850, and the unit filled immediately.

I was amazed, and I had additional cash flow. Remember what I said about keeping up with your marketplace and knowing it like it's the back of your hand? That's exactly what I was doing. I lived close by and worked the neighborhood, I talked with the neighbors, and I followed the data. Because of the additional cash flow, I began to rethink my mortgage situation. What if the properties were worth more money now? Should I refinance them? I had planned on keeping them for the long haul... but what if the bank would refinance them for $40,000 each? The additional rent would cover the additional payment, and I would have another $30,000 to go invest in other properties.

And guess what? The interest rates were lower at the time, resulting in my payment hardly changing. I'll take a deal like that all day long, same cash flow and receiving $30,000. No worries about a tax consequence; you don't pay tax until you sell the property. Refinance all you want, because there's no tax consequence.

Because I saw the trends, both on the map and in my immediate area, but also because no one was yet talking about this specific area, I had a hunch. And that hunch was, by continuing to purchase those distressed properties, I would increase my cash flow. And from my increased cash flow, I could continue renovating and paying my own bills. Lastly, with time, the value of the entire neighborhood would go up.

It was still a risk, but one I felt confident would pay off with the existing financial resources I had at my fingertips. Not only was I confident in my assessment, it represented an informed financial decision based on the cycles of my market. No fancy financial terms, and no over-complicated essays by ivory tower intellectuals.

Many years passed uneventfully with these units. The rent was paid, and I raised rents eventually to $1,200. I then put the money in my account, and every once in a while, I sent a repairman over to fix something. That was until the year 2000, when I started receiving calls from neighbors.

You see, originally, my tenants were the norm for the neighborhood. But the neighborhood was changing, and now my tenants did not please the neighbors.

"How interesting is that?" I thought.

So, I called a girlfriend and convinced her and her husband to buy the adjacent four units in the multi-unit buildings. When they did, we skipped renewing the existing leases, emptied the buildings, and began to renovate. Up until that point, I had done some renovating, but my girlfriend, Kathleen Turner—no, not *Romancing the Stone* Kathleen Turner, if you're familiar with that movie. More like Romancing the Home, Kathleen Turner! She had an awesome decorating ability. With her as an ally, we added second baths, historic moldings, new kitchens, the first use of granite at the time, stainless steel appliances, re-stuccoed the exterior, and landscaped to complete the picture. Our primary contractor, a partner who will serve a pivotal role later on in our story, even won an architectural preservation award from the city of St. Paul for all the work.

What was the result?

The homes were eventually sold for $235,000 and $215,000 each in 2001. Quite a return on investment! I wish that I could do this all the time, and when you continue to work the field, you'll have homeruns, just not every single time! Now, upon selling them, I would have had to pay Uncle Sam a lot of money, but because I was smart, I didn't need to. By then, I figured out how to do 1031 Tax-Deferred Exchanges. I sold both properties and bought seven duplexes, exchanging in my $664 cash flow for over $4,600 cash flow with seven appreciating assets instead of two.

Even though my initial purchases in this area were strategic financially-speaking, this set of decisions confirmed to me that I was indeed on a track few others could see at the time. That feeling was at once a little scary, but also an incredibly eye-opening moment into what financial freedom looked like.

If this much was possible, how much more was there, and how many opportunities were other people not seeing?

Frequently Asked Questions

Q: How did you know that it was the right time to take this level of risk?
A: At this point, I was taking smaller steps as I tested what would go on to be my larger theory and approach to wealth creation. Every single decision was made with my overall cash flow in mind, and if you're sensing a theme with that idea, you'd be exactly right.

Q: When you toured the properties, did you look for anything specific?
A: Over the years, I've had countless clients ask me what I specifically look for in each property. Whether it's a first-time home buyer with a family or an investor searching for rental properties, my answer is always the same: the ability to leverage increased potential against current value. I try and be open when I view each property. As you can see, these row houses, with their quirky charm, had this in abundance, even if they needed extra polish. I like to look at what's keeping others from being interested. Then I find a way to fix the problem and overcome the objection. In doing so, I generally improve the value of the home. Now, some features aren't fixable. But did I tell you that I *love* mold, termites, hoarder homes, and boarded windows? These spell "MONEY."

Do you have a property or two you have your eye on, but aren't sure about all the specifics? After buying and selling countless properties across the country, I love connecting one-on-one to provide my expert advice, so you can maximize your investor potential. Simply stop to my site to schedule an individual session now using this link:

http://www.TerryandJason.com/Apply

Q: I've been told that working with tenants can be difficult. What is your top advice for having tenants?
A: We'll talk a bit more about having tenants a few chapters from now, but my experience has been that the far majority of tenants are good people who, when respected, are more than willing to care for your investment. However, you can count on 5% of tenants being nightmares. It's horrible if your first experience as an investor is one of them. We'll give you tips to try and avoid being a statistic. I think it's good to learn how to manage your own tenants, but if it's not something you're interested in, hire a good property manager.

Insider's Tip

Every market will be different. There's no singular rule or principle in identifying a sound investment. We'll see later how intelligent strategies can help us make informed risks but realize that every single situation involves its own factors. This is why it's so critical to be connecting the dots on your own. The most important factor in finding an investment is identifying *your* goals. If you haven't set a clear path for your goals, you risk buying something you "like," but which doesn't help you achieve your goal.

CHAPTER 6

FINANCING & RESTOCKING YOUR SEED CORN

When you start on the road to financial freedom, it can be tempting for you to "eat your seed corn" before you've fully secured your freedom. In this chapter, we'll look at one of our most important concepts in attaining your vision and safeguarding your future.

In this chapter, you'll learn about:

- The ways your greater vision factors into your decisions
- Defining your "seed corn" and refining your financial plan
- Why liquidity can help you get further on your path
- How you can differentiate yourself from other people in the marketplace

So, what is "seed corn," and why does it matter for your finances? If you're like most new investors, you only have so much cash. That's it, a finite amount of cash. The most limiting factor for many of my investors is the amount of cash they possess to work with. And remember, for me, I only had $5,000. But I took an educated risk and bought two properties with that money and a credit card. Then, I worked like mad to earn the money to pay for the rehab.

For many people, their investment story would end here because they would have forgotten to develop a plan to re-stock their seed corn. In many cases, they might have spent it all and don't have a way to get it back. Re-stocking your seed corn ranks up there as one of the most important concepts we'll talk about.

The basic idea is that you need a strategy to get your cash back after you complete your project or you're done! So, for my first investment, I searched until I found a bank willing to finance my row houses for $25,000 a piece, giving me back my precious seed corn. Now, with my seed corn in hand,

I was free to go plant my seeds again and grow a new crop. Another strategy could have been to sell the properties. However, in this case, it didn't fit my goals. By keeping my goals in mind, I knew that using the units differently would achieve my initial goal of covering my car payment. If I sold them, no cash flow.

Others commonly make the following mistake with their newly-found seed corn after experiencing initial success: Porsche. Rolex. Gucci. You probably recognize these world-famous luxury brands, and you probably also know how attractive some of their products can be. Beyond those, there are many others that impress the crowds; you might even be able to name a number of them. And without question, they can be tempting when you first start your journey to financial freedom. This fact is true for just about everyone, no matter what your background is.

However, you've probably heard a story or two about everyone from famous musicians to lotto winners—individuals who became wealthy, splurged their money to excess, and then ended up broker than when they started. These extreme examples highlight a much-needed lesson at this stage of our journey to wealth creation; that lesson is on "re-stocking your seed corn."

Just like those famous musicians or lotto winners, when you start to attain financial freedom, you have access to newfound wealth. This wealth can take the form of quite a bit of liquid cash, available credit, and assets which may increase in value over time. In some cases, these can represent an unbelievable amount of money, even amounts you never thought you'd possess. With them comes the temptation to spend... and spend and spend. The next thing you know, you go to take stock of your financial resources, so you can jump on another opportunity, and you find... there's nothing left.

Back to square one. Your cash flow has dried up, and you're limited in your options.

Exhausting your seed corn, those financial resources that allow you to seize new opportunities and live the lifestyle you want, will put you back exactly where you started. After you've tasted even a bit of financial freedom, this feeling can be incredibly frustrating. But there's a better way, one where you enjoy your lifestyle, attain your vision, and stay in the investment game.

What could this previously unknown, magic secret be? I'm very glad you asked... If you're going to spend money, you should know how you're going to get it back. That's it!

Now, before you ask me, I want to be clear that I'm not saying you *must* skip the Porsche or the Rolex. Or any number of luxuries you may want to take advantage of. However, you certainly don't want to do so right now and not all the time at every opportunity. Because, the fact of the matter is that your vision should drive your decisions, instead of letting your impulses or quick rewards do so.

As we re-stock our seed corn, finding ways to get back our investments, we're always re-positioning ourselves for wealth generation, instead of consuming all our wealth all at once. This approach is one that I cannot stress enough in my seminars. In today's day and age, we're almost conditioned to spend our seed corn immediately, instead of funneling it back into our wealth creation and long-term happiness. Nothing could be more detrimental to attaining your vision for financial freedom.

Sure, it means that sometimes, you have to sacrifice one reward to attain a later one. For many of us, it also means you have to decide what type of person you are. You can be organized, methodical, decisive, and deliberative about your finances and your future. Or you can spend all that initial reward the moment you get it. The choice is always yours, but your vision of financial freedom only allows for one of these. Far too often, I've seen someone get the taste of freedom, only to waste their seed corn and grow frustrated when they have to start all over. Many even wasted their seed corn on the thrill of investing, without having a clear plan for how they would get their cash back.

When it comes down to it, you'll also find that nearly everyone is ready to get you to spend your seed corn. That real estate agent who you're working with? I hate to say it, but in many cases, they see your 25% down and just want to sell you a duplex. For plenty of people, that's perfectly fine.

But, if you're reading this book, you're not "plenty of people," and you have something else in mind.

The truth is, if you value attaining financial freedom, you want to have a vision for how you'll get your cash back. During my experience purchasing Dale Street properties, I learned that, if I put in $25k, I wanted to get that cash back by refinancing, for example. Then I also wanted to increase my rental income, if possible and where appropriate; I wanted to pay my car payment and my house payment at the end of the month (and this was only the start).

If I had merely spent the money, without a second thought, I wouldn't have had the luxury of the future I saw for myself. So, please, please, *please*, do not eat your seed corn, not at the start and not later either. As you raise your financial freedom, you'll see how you can even channel your passion for more expensive hobbies into wealth creation as well. It can be hard to believe, but it's completely true as we'll see later on in the book.

A final word on real estate agents, if I may. After decades in the business and in investing, I feel that I can speak from a position of expert authority on this topic. There are many fine agents out there, but for every good one, there's one who is less than ideal. For you, on your journey to financial freedom, you'll want to find the right real estate agent. During my journey, I had the luxury of being my own real estate agent at a time when the industry was still changing. For wealth creation, your relationship with your agent should be founded on strategic finances and identifying your goals.

Frequently Asked Questions

Q: What are some of the lesser-known values or strategies that served you best in your personal journey to financial freedom?

A: I would say that doing right by the people around me always helped me in a number of ways. Whether it was my tenants who were safeguarding my investments, my contractors who provided me their best advice, or later, my partners who supported me in raising the bar further, respecting them and appreciating them for their hard work was instrumental. They motivated me and made it all possible.

Q: Do factors like my credit score matter as much as people say?

A: In real estate, people are always asking about their credit scores. Although it definitely is an important piece of your financial puzzle, it is not nearly as important as people make it out to be. We'll see later in our story how others I've worked with were able to overcome even the worst scores.

Q: Should you avoid a decision that doesn't allow you to get your money back?

A: In most cases, yes. If you can't see a clear path to restocking your seed corn, you should be very skeptical of that financial decision.

Insider's Tip

Understand that everybody has a pitch, and in many cases, something they're trying to sell. There's nothing inherently wrong with this, as you can identify those pitches that can help you obtain your own goals. When you're talking with a real estate agent or financial source, ask how their service is benefiting your vision or what value they provide you on your journey.

CHAPTER 7

BUILDING A TEAM

Even if you consider yourself a leader and a self-starter, this chapter walks you through the necessity of refining your team building skills. On your road to financial freedom, you'll come to rely on many people from disparate industries and walks of life. Being able to put together the team you trust can mean the difference between getting the job done right or not at all.

In this chapter, you'll learn about:
- How broad your professional network will need to be
- The risks of choosing the wrong people
- Resisting the urge to micro-manage your team
- Finding the pros and identifying them
- Keeping them in your network

How much do you know about doing your taxes? Maybe a fair amount. What about mortgage title insurance or rental leads? How well can you wire an electrical outlet or replace the plumbing for a bathtub?

When you start investing, you may be tempted to think that you can do it all or at least a lot of it. But from my first Dale Street property to my 100th property, I knew that there was more involved than simply painting a wall here or slapping on a new fixture there. Part of it was because these properties needed their own share of work, from windows upgrades to walling. Still, there's a bit more to the story.

From the start, I knew that I would need a team of experts. Although I could have prepared the taxes myself or cleaned out the units the first time on my own, I knew that the problem was two-fold. First, in any one unit, there could be a number of different upgrades needed. Instead of learning a new skill or refining my own, I wanted people who wouldn't just get the job done. In reality, I wanted people who wouldn't need to do the job a second time. Or a third time. And all because they hadn't done it right initially.

However, it also came down to time. If I was taking time to struggle to learn all the ins and outs of restoring hardwood floors, for example, I was taking time away from understanding my market. Or seeking out new opportunities. Not only will you need to know a broad array of skills for your investing, you won't have the time to master them all. This fact is certainly true when it comes to the professional who is obsessed with perfecting their own skill or field, from roofing to bookkeeping.

At the same time, you'll still want to be a "semi-expert" in everything. What that means is that you should be able to keep up in a conversation with the professional, but then know when to get out of the way and let them do what they do best. First-time investors can be especially inclined to micro-manage their teams to the point of disaster, but I'll caution you to "sit on your fingers."

The pitfalls of choosing the wrong professionals can be huge as well. When I was still putting together my team during those Dale Street days, I had a heating company rip me off, for example. Even after doing my due diligence, they decided to cut and run one day. For me, this was a powerful lesson in assessing the skills and values of anyone I would hire in the future. While it may cost a few more dollars to hire the right people the first time, doing so can save you even more time, money, and more importantly, save you from headaches that open you up to more risk.

So, now that we know how important putting together a team of experts can be, how do we find the pros? Better yet, how do we keep them in our network once we've found them?

One thing I learned during those early days on Dale Street, and an approach that would serve me well to this day, is to talk with each candidate myself. Of course, I first had to find them, and the easiest way to accomplish that task was to go where they were. In almost every case, professionals in every field have organizations they belong to, places they seek out new opportunities themselves, or even just places they hang out together.

And professionals talk. In fact, you're probably not surprised to find out that they get to know each other very well. The owner of that flooring company I worked with on Dale Street? Professionals like them know exactly who to trust when it comes to, for example, re-doing all the cabinets in the kitchens. If you work with someone who shows that they are absolutely committed to providing value, ask them who they recommend for other projects.

And this strategy is also wonderful for keeping those same professionals in your network for the long haul. As you start to get a name for yourself as a person who's hard-working and perceptive when it comes to investing, recommend your professionals to others. Talk them up! You'll find that this strengthens those relationships beyond measure.

Going back to what I mentioned about talking to them yourself, however... by sitting down with your candidates yourself, you can gauge a whole host of factors. Whether you're asking them about their commitment to their clients or talking with them about the best methods for getting a job done, you don't have to filter their answers through a third-party. You also have the chance to ask them those tougher questions about how they may have handled a more challenging job or one that didn't go as expected. These insights give you a window into whether this person will do just enough or go the mile in making your vision a reality.

But let's relate these lessons and tips on teams back to the real world. During my time on Dale Street and for the following decades, my teams have helped make my financial freedom possible. On the one hand, I was identifying the opportunities and taking the risk. On the other hand, my teams have risen to the occasion in transforming those "diamonds in the rough" into assets that other investors envy. By clearing a way for my professionals to do what they did best, I was able to attain my vision and generate wealth along the way.

When you build a team founded on this philosophy, it will truly make your road to financial freedom a better experience.

What have been your major concerns for your team? I'd love to talk about the possibilities; simply visit my site to book an individual coaching session now and we can discuss your journey to financial freedom:

http://www.TerryandJason.com/Apply

Frequently Asked Questions

Q: What are some of the other best ways to keep the pros in your network once you've identified them?
A: Always recognize when your professionals have done a job that exceeded your expectations. This tip not only sets the stage for them to do so again in the future, but it also shows them how you pay attention to the details and recognize when they've mastered the craft they love.
Q: Really, what's the difference in a team that's "okay" versus one consisting of pros?
A: A great deal of time and money, in all honesty. An okay team might come in and get the job done, mostly meet your requirements, but completely miss your deadline, for example. In the world of investing, that lost time can delay other parts of the process, and in the end, cost you an opportunity.

Q: What happens when one of my team members isn't meeting my expectations or my vision?
A: As a leader, I go to that team member and ask them what's going on. That discussion might feel confrontational when you're just beginning to put your team together, but in every case, clearly re-conveying my expectations while removing any obstacle in the team member's path, if I could,

has served me well. However, if you've given them a couple opportunities already, never feel bad about switching to someone else. Your financial freedom depends on it.

Insider's Tip

The team you start out with doesn't necessarily have to be the team you have in a decade. In fact, as you increase your wealth, your current team will lead you to your next team. This outlook means that you're always refining your existing team as you discover better and better professionals.

CHAPTER 8

FIRST TENANT

This chapter delves into how all the people around you, not just your team members, become investors in your vision, either directly or indirectly. By recognizing how essential they are to the process, you'll be setting up yourself for even more success on your journey to financial freedom.

In this chapter, you'll learn about:

- Recognizing people's pain points and their rewards
- Property management's challenges, but also, its benefits
- How having higher expectations leads to positive outcomes
- What to do when you have a less-than-ideal tenant

B efore we move on to our next investment purchases, we have just one more lesson to learn from my time on Dale Street. Because your first financial steps represent one of the most critical times during your journey, we need to ensure we have a few pieces in place first. This section deals with our next piece of the wealth generation puzzle: managing tenants and how they also greatly factor into your vision.

If you have any existing familiarity with property management or have known someone who has been a landlord, you may have heard endless horror stories. Tenants who wouldn't pay, tenants who ruined the home, tenants who disappeared. If you were to take these at face value, you might wonder why anyone would rent out a piece of property.

Still, my experience, from Dale Street onward, was totally different.

Remember, because I viewed my tenants as co-investors in my vision, I approached the situation with a novel outlook. Instead of viewing them as simply tenants who I collected rent from each month, I saw them as those people who were safeguarding my investments while I was away. So, what did this look like?

I got to know each of my tenants. During conversations, I would learn what their challenges were but also what motivated them. Early on, I would pick up and deliver turkeys to their homes for Thanksgiving. I even remember one particularly warm year in Minnesota when my truck was full of turkeys, and I feared they would all thaw out. Alongside me, my kids were helping me go from door-to-door delivering them. The tenants were very appreciative and even expressed gratitude dozens of years later when they call looking for a new rental.

And that's not all we did. In many cases, our early tenants were single parents on welfare. So, during the holidays, we would buy "Toys for Tots" gifts for them. If something broke in their unit, you better believe that I was on the phone with my expert team the moment I had a chance. Finally, we treated our tenants so good from the very beginning, they were more than willing to treat our properties exceptionally well.

"Treat the janitor with as much respect as you would treat the CEO" is a motto I intended to live by. If I was entrusting these individuals with my investments and ability to produce cash flow, I knew that I couldn't afford to do otherwise. And what were the benefits?

Well, I can share stories of wealth creation with you, stories of financial freedom. I can also share stories of working with numerous professionals to get major projects finished. Beyond those, I can even share stories with you like ones where we delivered turkeys to my tenants during St. Paul's most brutal winters.

What I can't share with you are the type of horror stories you hear from others, because I don't really have any of those.

Don't get me wrong; I did experience a less-than-ideal tenant or two over the years. Like I said before, there is a percentage of tenants that can be a challenge. And in a moment, we'll talk about how to handle those situations. However, on the whole, by treating people with dignity and respect, you'll gain allies everywhere you go. This fact is as much true if you're talking to investors in the boardroom of a bank, reviewing plans with contractors on the construction site for new condos, or connecting with your tenants in your own properties.

The fact of the matter is that people of every background want respect. Whether they've lived in Southwest Florida or San Diego, this statement is equally true. And after decades working with tenants, I can positively say that showing genuine respect for who they were as people has gone a long way.

So, what do you do when you find yourself with a less-than-ideal tenant? It didn't happen often for me, and I can only remember it being an issue maybe once or twice. On the whole, I found that most tenants were good people, and for every one that was less-than-ideal, ten more were completely amazing.

Of course, if someone does lose your respect, you don't entrust them with your biggest assets. You also must be ready to be tough and direct. For those of you who are new to investing or leadership roles, this approach can also feel confrontational on the surface. However, if you don't convey clear expectations or let it slide that someone isn't meeting yours, a tenant could possibly take advantage and ruin your property from the ground up.

Do not misinterpret "treating them well" to mean be "easy" or as their "best friend." You must treat your investments as a business and consistently and firmly uphold the rules. If they view you as too soft, they will take advantage of you and the circumstances. Instead, hold the line and earn their respect. Rent is due on the first; you must be paid first. If you make allowances, you'll always be paid second or last.

You can probably see now why I stress so much that respect is key. Your tenants are safeguarding a strategic piece of your vision, and you should treat them like it. If one of them isn't meeting that expectation, there's ten more good-willed people lined up behind them who need a place to live. Don't hesitate to directly and confidently rectify any issues.

Over time, even if that directness feels odd for you at first, you'll find that your tenants appreciate you for it. After all, if you don't tell your tenants what you need from them, how will they know? They can't read your mind and may have completely different expectations than you do about your investments.

And for you, those investments are pivotal for attaining financial freedom.

Frequently Asked Questions

Q: I've had real estate agents tell me property management can be too difficult to become involved in. Do you recommend it as a financial choice?

A: Remember when we said everyone has an agenda? While I wouldn't necessarily recommend property management to a complete novice or without a mentor, you can see from my personal story that I made it work.

Q: What laws should I know about when it comes to property management?

A: An excellent question! For property management, you'll want to read up on a number of laws, so you can ensure you're always in compliance. While there are more than a few of them, they aren't overly complicated, but I also recommend partnering with a mentor to understand these better.

Q: How do you identify a flip from a rental property?

A: In Chapter 12, we'll look at the finer points on distinguishing when to flip, rent, or run, as well as in my subsequent book. Bottom-line is which circumstances better allow you to get your cash back and what the current market is doing.

Insider's Tip

Don't become attached to your rental properties any more than you would become attached to your principal residence. Staying objective is one of the foremost principals to staying on the path to financial freedom.

Have an issue you need an objective opinion on? You always have a resource in me, and all you need to do is schedule a one-on-one session for us, and we can take a look at where you're at right now:

http://www.TerryandJason.com/Apply

CHAPTER 9
BEGINNING TO CREATE MOMENTUM

This chapter takes us from our initial vision of wealth creation to where we can glimpse at the real possibilities. We've identified what's working and how we should capitalize on it, but now, we're at a strategically critical point. For this chapter, we'll identify your direction and how not to miss out on increasing its momentum earlier than I originally did.

In this chapter, you'll learn about:

- Dreaming bigger than you could have imagined at first
- Working with your goals and vision in the bigger picture
- Spending the time to get to your financial freedom
- Evaluating, evaluating, evaluating

I 'm going to be completely honest... when it comes to the 7th through 10th properties and beyond, it's hard to remember them all.

However, I continued to acquire properties with the same working principals I had started out with. For example, from the Dale Street properties, about 18 months later, I would go on to find a single family, 2-bedroom home in another area few were interested in investing in. This piece of real estate was located at 1166 Thomas Ave. Personally, I liked the area, as the first home I owned when married was in this neighborhood. However, the bank thought very differently.

And like my other properties, this home needed some love, to say the least. There was no heat, the windows were boarded up, and hardwood flooring needed sanding. Just picture it for a moment, if you can: an older bungalow style craftsman home, completely empty, boarded up, and who could tell what else was wrong because the power wasn't on.

There weren't any investors lining up to acquire this one, and there certainly weren't any real estate agents showing it off. Everyone assumed that there had been vandalism to the home because the windows were boarded. I thought it was funny at the time, because, having lived in the neighborhood, I couldn't imagine someone breaking out the windows in this location, so I looked closer. Armed with my flashlight and my handyman from Dale St, we carefully examined the home.

What did we find?

The windows were intact underneath! The asset manager for the bank who owned it had ordered someone to board the windows. This action alone decreased the value based on perception and by probably $20,000, in my opinion. Their loss was my gain!

I saw the potential in it, and the genuine enjoyment a young family, for example, might get from it. And when I purchased it for $10k, I knew exactly what I was going to do to upgrade it and get my cash back. So, I sanded the floors, removed the plywood, shined the original, wavy glass windows, painted, and completed the rehab. Then I went on to find a suitable tenant.

Now, the most important action: replacing my seed corn. I contacted my bank and arranged to place financing on the property. I received a loan of $40,000 on it, obtaining my original purchase money and fix-up expenses plus some extra cash, all while still obtaining cash flow of $332 per month on the home after I paid my monthly expenses.

And later? Well, much later on, I would even sell this home for roughly $100,000 in less than ten years. However, the main point is that I knew how to restock my seed corn and off I went again.

In reality, I had developed my own model.

My first project took me 18 months to complete; my second deal took 6 months. Why the change? I was getting better at the process. And the following purchases after seven were a blur. Because I now possessed the answers I needed for most problems, I didn't have to research each time there was a problem. I just proceeded ahead, finding good deals, purchasing them, getting them "rent ready," renting them, and eventually re-financing them to obtain seed corn. The speed with which I went was determined by the cash I had in hand.

For my properties, I self-managed my own until I finally hit 28 units. When the rental calls started interfering with my "job" of earning money selling homes to other people, I hired someone to manage my units. At the time, I didn't trust anyone else with my hard-earned assets. In my real estate career, I've seen how poorly other management companies managed their client units. So, I hired someone and taught them what I wanted them to do and was still in control on the sidelines.

And because I like to make strategic decisions on my properties, based on the overall long-term goal of property, there was another factor. If an improvement needs to be made, I like to make one that will increase the value of the home, if possible. Contrary to what you might hear, the cheapest fix is not always the best.

But think about all the regular tasks to managing a property. Ensuring rent is collected, placing those calls to have a couch removed, reviewing the everyday details. All those "15 minute" tasks can really add up when you're talking about multiplying them across many units, let alone if something urgent comes up. When you need the help of a property management company, choose one that treats your property like they own it personally. You'll then be able to focus on the task of identifying new projects and building wealth. It's important to know the details of how to do property management, but once you've mastered it, let someone else do it. Your job as an investor is a higher pay grade!

From there, I wondered just how far I could go. What was the limit to what started out on that cold St. Paul day when I looked at my first Dale Street property?

Around this time or right before it, I went to lunch with my calculator. Remember, I had covered my car payment and my house payment. Now what? And I thought back to what I had heard people like David Knox, an early pioneer real estate agent, say about dreaming.

"Dream bigger" was the gist of the advice I had heard, but there was more to it. "Bigger and better. There was no limit if you were smart and strategic about it."

Then I started doing the numbers and asking myself questions. Remember how important I said that it was to ask yourself questions and be constantly evaluating? That's exactly what I was doing, even after I had enjoyed those initially successes. There isn't a point where you should stop evaluating where you are or what resources you have at your disposal.

So, think about it for a moment. What if I did 30 units? What about 50? Finally, what if I went for 100 units?

There I was, thinking and running the numbers at lunch on a regular day. Around me, the world was bustling with noise, and people were caught up in their own affairs. Yet, it didn't even feel like work to me, because I was thinking about my vision. Little did I know, I was about to discover my own breakthrough into how limitless the possibilities really are when it comes to wealth creation.

A bit later, and we'll talk about this a bit more in the next chapter, I would sit down and create a spreadsheet to compare and contrast the numbers. Even though I had already added up the numbers myself in the past, this was the moment I realized how wealth creation was a process, and it could be scaled up. By doing so, you could also analyze the outcomes of different scenarios; say, if your rents continued at their current pace, how that would affect your cash flow per month.

With that spreadsheet, I would figure out my annual depreciation on the units I owned (which leads to tax savings), the various possibilities for my monthly cash on hand, and my total return on investment. I was also able to discover how I could adapt my situation as needed to retain my wealth and grow it even bigger.

Today, I aptly call this sheet my Dream Sheet.

Because your vision can be a bigger picture idea you might have, you also have to be willing to drill down and pair it with the details. In this case, as I moved beyond simply having a handful of properties, it became more critical to unite these two factors. What I found was that my vision could have been much, much different from the very start.

Forget just paying your car payment or your house payment, because we're talking about something much, much different and unbelievable.

I spent those next few weeks dreaming bigger and bigger. At the same time, I continued to crunch the numbers, considering possibilities. Instead of fighting against how my view was changing and insisting that my vision was only one possibility, I seized on the idea that there were many, many possibilities.

The more time I spent doing this activity of dreaming about my vision, the more time I spent figuring out how I would get there. In reality, the jump from having a couple properties under your belt to 30, 40, or even 100 is just as much about your vision as it is the details. Once you've started to master the other principles we've been talking about, all you need do next is dream bigger.

And I mean, bigger than you first thought ever possible. Still, there's one more critical piece you have to add.

Once you dream bigger, then you dream better by putting in the time evaluating what you'll need to do and then by doing it.

Frequently Asked Questions

Q: How big is dreaming too big when it comes to my financial freedom?
A: As long as you're dreaming better and putting in the time, there's no limit to your vision. Once you realize this fact and commit to overcoming the challenges, you'll see what I mean. I only wish I had dreamt bigger from the very start like you can now!

Q: What's the best way to keep track of your vision as it grows and changes?
A: Everyone has their own way of keeping track of their dreams. Although I recommend keeping a spreadsheet of the numbers, which we'll touch on again later, you can keep a motivation list or a vision journal. I've seen people hang images of their biggest desires as a way of keeping their goals front and center. For me, at present, I have my Dream Board in my hallway on the wall, and I'm in the process of making a large blackboard wall in my office, so I can write my goals on the wall large enough for myself and others to take in at all times. You see, if you have a goal, and you share it with others and review your goal daily, you are ten times more likely to achieve your dream or goal.

Q: What tricks or tips can you give me to getting better at evaluating?

A: Practice, first of all. With experience, patience, and observation, you'll soon see how an old solution to a different problem can be adapted for the current day, for example. I would also recommend getting an experienced mentor who can provide you with further advice. Whether you review your past choices with them or alone, you'll be way ahead of 99% of people when it comes to financial situations. Also, look at hundreds and then thousands of properties.

Insider's Tip

Seek out motivations that keep you focused on your vision. Because the goal of financial freedom doesn't happen overnight, you'll go through a range of emotions during your journey. You don't want to get discouraged, and as long as you don't eat your seed corn, as we talked about in Chapter 6, you should be good.

CHAPTER 10
BEGINNING TO CREATE MY OWN MODEL

For this chapter, we'll start piecing together how you can go from basic strategies and momentum to a full model, even if no one else is doing what you're doing. We've seen just how important it can be to fully evaluate your situation, but now, we'll look at how I refined that process. You'll also see how you can implement your model sooner to achieve your financial freedom on an even faster timeline than I did.

In this chapter, you'll learn about:
- Refining your vision further by creating a complete model
- The need to not "re-create the wheel every single time"
- How other investing books aren't written until opportunities have passed
- Why this book is different and how my coaching factors into that mission

At the end of the day, there's no magic formula.

By this point, I hope you're getting the sense of how wealth creation isn't easy in and of itself. In reality, a lot of thought and work go into it, from the moment you hire your first contractor to the time you spend crunching numbers. But equally true is the fact that it's not a magical process that only the experts have locked away, sharing the secrets only with each other.

Wealth creation, and in turn, financial freedom, is as much what you put into it as what you can take out of it.

With that spreadsheet, my Dream Sheet, I would be able to figure out a few components I was missing in my journey. This period and that tool were the start of what I would call "refining my model," solidifying it as a method I could repeat over and over again. Just like a doctor evaluating a patient and determining the best current course of action for their health, I was synthesizing my experiences into a complete model.

First, I needed a sense of my "annual depreciation" on the units I owned. This aspect may be well-known to some of you, but many of you might not have seen it before. We'll look more in detail at this tax-related strategy and a few others in an upcoming chapter, but right now, all you need know is that you're allowed to factor in depreciation in a property over time on your taxes. In turn, you can save some serious cash.

I also went on to calculate various possibilities for my monthly cash on hand. Recall from our previous chapter, our example was what would happen if rents continued at their current pace. Yet, there are a number of other relationships, all basically easy to understand once you get the hang of them, that you can determine at this point in your journey.

And really, these relationships are just you asking questions about what you've seen in your investments. What is your total return on investment? How quickly are you re-stocking your seed corn? How are your single-family homes in one part of town comparing to your row houses on the other side of town?

By drawing out a few important relationships from the data, I was able to see an entirely new world. I was also able to discover how I could adapt my situation as needed to retain my wealth and grow it even bigger and better.

How amazing does that sound?

Now, if you're just dying to know all the details of what was on my Dream Sheet, you don't have to worry. In Chapter 11, I'm going to share it with you *absolutely free*, and we'll talk a bit more about how you can use it to gain even more momentum on your journey. This way, you can start building wealth even sooner and more quickly than I did.

However, there's a number of important takeaways from this point in my financial journey. Of course, we've seen how evaluating your situation can be taken to the next level. And yet, all we're doing is asking questions!

Still, by refining my model and creating a spreadsheet to track my investments, I was able to make decisions more objectively, instead of subjectively. For example, when determining how extensively to rehab a unit, I needed to consider what my long-term strategy was for each property. If I added a new kitchen to a property, sometimes the property would support increased rents and sometimes not. Another consideration before making a major improvement decision is the after-repaired value of the property. Will the property be worth more after you do the improvement? Does the cost of the renovation improve the value of the property equal to or more than the cost? If so, it could be a good improvement. If not, it is probably an unnecessary improvement. Over time, by incorporating these strategies into my plan, I developed a model to follow and was less likely to make improvements based on my personal "wants" but in line with my own personal investment model.

Following that same line of thought, you can also get rid of what's not working and keep what's working. Just like a coach honing a team for the championship, we want to see how even the smallest details funnel back into our vision for great things. If we skipped this step, like the team forgetting to practice regularly, we'd be missing the chance of a lifetime.

A further word on coaching... at the time I was creating this spreadsheet, no one else was doing what I was doing. There were no books on the subject, and I couldn't just read up on what to do. There were also no gurus with slick websites, and even fewer of my peers were seeing what I was seeing. In fact, everyone in real estate was sick of rentals, and no one wanted anything to do with them.

And that was a good thing. It meant more opportunities for me, and it forced me to connect the dots all on my own, connecting them in my market and for my resources. It also allowed me to create a model that would serve me well, from those initial units to millions of dollars. Most importantly, no one was there trying to sell me a magic formula for financial freedom.

That's where this book comes in. At this point, you're probably starting to understand that you can draw from my personal experiences to adapt them to your own. Unlike the gurus and the salespeople, I'm giving you my tools, but also letting you know that you can modify them, expand on them, and refine them even more.

I also know how difficult it can be not having a trusted mentor you can turn to, someone who can give you advice about your specific situation. Because of this fact, I am constantly giving seminars and coaching other investors and real estate agents on wealth creation and financial freedom. However, the most important part is that I also provide coaching and mentorship for investors and agents, no matter where they are on their journey. This way, you can skip the magic formulas everyone else is selling, the get-rich-quick schemes, and get actionable advice custom tailored for your vision.

With all of these resources, you'll also be able to attain your goals on a faster timetable than I was.

Frequently Asked Questions

Q: How do you know if your model is a good one?
A: First of all, my model was founded on years of experience and many situations. However, there's more to the story. Your model is a way of looking at the world, not necessarily a prediction machine. With it, you can tease out what you believe has worked in the past and what will likely continue to work. It's a way to see beyond any one fact, and a way to filter out the noise. Does it help you see the details and the bigger picture? Then it's a good one.

Q: How do you really know what's working and what isn't?

A: It can be hard, in the moment, to identify this. That's why evaluating over the long term and short term is important. With your model, you'll be able to crunch the hard numbers to see where you're losing money, for example, as much as you'll be able to see where you can shift your investments for better cash flow.

Q: If refining your model was so important to your vision, are you still doing so to this day?
A: Yes! Although I can now enjoy mentoring investors and real estate agents, I still regularly test the assumptions of my own model. After all, the same values that started me on this journey are still serving me well to this day.

Insider's Tip

As we saw earlier, the road to your financial freedom is paved with astonishingly diverse skills. Many people focus on only one or two and to the detriment of the others. Think of your journey as one where you'll be required to trust your gut but temper your impulses with proper planning, one that requires risk but not blind risk without thought. My model helped me to tame the situation, and I continued to look at my spreadsheet on a daily basis.

CHAPTER 11

STRATEGIC GOAL PLANNING & DREAM SHEET

We've heard a bit about it now, but in this chapter, you'll gain access to my Dream Sheet. We're also going to outline how you can formalize your strategic goal planning to take better advantage of your situation. This way, you'll be able to get organized and see your path more clearly.

In this chapter, you'll learn about:

- Strategically breaking down your goal
- Discovering answers to the most important questions
- How sacrificing one factor leads to an even greater one
- The essential need to pair up with a mentor

Should I dream bigger?

Yes! Remember our FAQ from Chapter 9, where I said there isn't any limit to how big or how much better you can dream? I truly meant it. Let me give you an example of just what I mean.

When I first thought to put together my Dream Sheet, I was also wondering how big you should dream. Was there really no limit to what you could envision? So, I wrote down my monthly income goal, remembering what David Knox had taught me earlier. The first number I wrote down was $5,000. This number represented more than what I had made as an Occupational Therapist in the 1980s.

But then I remembered what David said again so, I crossed it off. And doubled it.

$10,000 in a month. Now, that seemed like a fair amount of cash to be generating for myself every month, after all other expenses were taken care of. With that much, I could spend all my time seeking out new opportunities and focusing on investment skills.

Still David was lurking in my consciousness, so again I crossed off that number. And doubled it again.

$20,000 a month in income for myself. It made my skin crawl. This number was more than I had ever imagined possible in a single month. Of course, now we do $20,000 in a month without even thinking, but at this stage of my journey into financial freedom, I understand that there's no limit to how big you can dream.

And now that we understand that you have to have the vision and the details, we're ready to really get down to business. Let's break down your financial journey into more detail and help you discover what your goals truly are, along with another lesson.

When I meet with each of my coaching clients, I personally ask them what their individual goals are. Then we start to break down those goals into strategic pieces. Your vision can be a powerful motivator and help you see the bigger picture, so it's one place I love to start out. Seeing the enthusiasm my clients have truly inspires me just as much as it does them.

So, what are your goals for financial freedom?

Do you want regular monthly income, for example? Or maybe you'd like income for your future retirement? What about proceeds from future sales to pay your children's way through college?

These questions illustrate a mere sample of the possibilities, but each question helps us get to the heart of your specific goals. And just like we discovered at the start of my journey, taking stock of your financial resources from there is a good place to launch your financial freedom.

How does your credit look? What is your current savings or traditional investments? Do you have a job?

You might think that last question sounds a little odd; at least, occasionally, some people in my seminars do. However, we'll soon find out that it's not all that uncommon for someone to start their journey into financial freedom without a stable job. And even in those situations, we can tap into other strategic finances to get you on your path to financial freedom. In every single situation with any client I've worked with, we've been able to identify their goals and determine what financial resources we could put into action.

From there, we determine what they need to sacrifice and what they need to do to attain their vision.

That word may sound a little scary at first— "sacrifice." But think of it like this: by giving up one thing, you attain another. Most importantly, by disposing of something you sort of want, you're able to grab something you want even more, *much* more.

And that's financial freedom, the ability to live on your terms and generate stable income.

Nothing highlights this situation better than a time in my own journey. After St. Paul and many years later, I would land in Montana. All my wealth creation had afforded me my dream home. I put the dishes on the shelves, as they say, and put up pictures of my most treasured moments. Without question, I can say that I never wanted to move again.

But there were only 35 foreclosures in Bozeman. So, I had to choose. Did owning my dream home matter to me as much as building my vision bigger and better?

I'll admit... it wasn't an easy choice. Yet, the power of wealth generation was that important to me, and it had captivated me. If I hadn't made this difficult decision, however, I may never have found out how my model could work in multiple locations at once. In a future chapter, we'll look at that approach in more detail.

Still, you can see why I recommend pairing up with a mentor during your financial journey, and one with plenty of experience. Having someone who's been there and made the same decisions can help give you a remarkable amount of perspective into your own situation.

For now, let's get you that Dream Sheet.

Frequently Asked Questions

Q: Where do you find a reliable mentor who you can trust?
A: I recommend connecting with a mentor who's experienced and upfront about their own vision for the future. It can be difficult to come by such a person regularly, and there's no one place where they "hang out." This is one reason I started offering my mentoring services.

Q: What makes a mentor better than just any regular professional?
A: Your mentor will assess *your* unique situation, and they provide you with sound resources. At the same time, they've been where you are and have experienced the same sorts of situations. This fact can lead to a wealth of concrete actions they can provide you specifically, but also, they understand where you're coming from.

Q: What if my situation isn't truly like anyone else's situation?

A: After mentoring hundreds of individuals and meeting countless more who attend my seminars, I feel confident that I can say I've seen a large percentage of investment situations. Sure, you may have one that's unlike any other, but remember, when I started out, just like everyone else, I had my own resources and my own market to understand. Bottom-line: you could say every situation is unique in its own way.

Insider's Tip

Writing down your goals and being specific about them is the most important thing you can do on your quest for much more in life. And the story of my Dream Sheet is interesting. Remember, before I met my now husband Jason, I used to go to lunch with my calculator. I figured out all the benefits of owning rentals and put them on paper. In doing so, I decided I would repeat the doubling exercise but now apply it to the number of units I owned. So, I started with 10, then 20, then 50 and finally I decided what the heck, and I created the sheet based on 100 units.

Eventually, after years and years, I become so good at the numbers, my subconsciousness took over. I had spent time visualizing the accomplishment, and all the information was part of my natural way of doing things. In the end, I would grow my portfolio to 100 units, not 99 and not 101. How interesting, I thought! Subconsciously, I found a way to complete my goals on my Dream Sheet. It was almost a decade later when I thought of the sheet again and realized the irony of it. And I'm going to share this resource with you now. However, you should create your own Dream Sheet with your average cash flow per unit and likely appreciation for your area.

In the meantime, however, I'm happy to share my Dream Sheet with you to get you started. All you'll need to do is use the following link to download it, *absolutely free*:

http://www.TerryandJason.com/Downloads

CHAPTER 12

FACTORING YOUR TAXES INTO YOUR JOURNEY TO FINANCIAL FREEDOM

This chapter walks you through some of the more advanced ways an investor might use to manage their tax situation. By doing so, you can make your taxes part of your strategic decisions, leading to better investment outcomes and stronger wealth generation.

In this chapter, you'll learn about:

- The need to regularly manage your taxes
- How the rewards of doing so can grow your financial freedom
- Common misconceptions about taxes
- Using 1031 Tax-Deferred Exchanges to your benefit

P rior to getting into real estate, I took an H&R Block income tax course while on bed rest with my second child. At the time, I was young, 25 years old, and didn't understand why we had to pay the government all that the money at the end of the year. But I knew that developing a deeper knowledge in this area would help me in the long term. So, I took the class, and through it, identified two ways to possibly reduce your taxes.

1. Grow your family by having more kids.

But I already had two, and that was enough for me. Or...

2. Own a rental property yourself

As I started building my portfolio, this seed of information had been in my head for three years. But by now, I owned lots of rental properties. However, the other thing I learned in that course was that the government was potentially going to take a large piece of my gain if I were to sell any property. So, although that really hadn't been a problem so far, it was something to think about. I had become good at purchasing rental properties, but not selling them, not yet anyway. And by purchasing these properties, they were off-setting the income from the "job" where I earned money for daily expenses.

You might wonder why I wouldn't have had a "gain" instead of a "loss," since these properties were cash flowing?

When you purchase rental properties, all costs and expenses including travel are deductible on your tax return. If you fix up a property, the cost is deductible, though some big items might be deducted over a few years, but that depends on current tax code.

I also call this the "Donald Trump Phenomena." For some people, they simply don't understand how he had losses. But the truth is, if he was acquiring, he had losses.

Since most of the properties I purchased needed work, I always had lots of deductions for repairs on my tax returns. Generally, I refinanced sometime in the first year in order to obtain my cash back. Remember restocking your seed corn? That's what I was doing. And refinancing is *not* a taxable event.

So, all the cash flow—cash left after paying monthly expenses per property, was off-set with all the purchasing as I continued to buy. But after taking the H&R Block classes, I knew that I was in trouble if I wanted to sell a property. If you sell a rental property, it's a taxable event; that is, unless you complete a 1031 Tax-Deferred Exchange. I had heard of them, but still, no one around me was savvy in this area, not at the time.

However, I kept my ears open and finally saw a course by Chris Bird about how to beat the IRS and pay less tax by utilizing Tax-Deferred Exchanges. Can you imagine what I did next? I took the courses! And afterward, I decide to use myself as a guinea pig.

Until just into the 2000s, I held all my purchases. But I knew I had a tax problem for Dale Street. You'll remember that I had bought each unit for $5,011, and by this time, they were worth *much* more.

Now, if I would outright sell the units, I would pay the IRS lots of money, losing much of my money. During this time, I had gotten in the habit of analyzing the annual cash-on-cash and total returns on investment for every property. The Dale Street properties held lots of equity for me, and the rent had increased. However, I was obtaining about $332 per unit in monthly cash flow, and I realized I could do better.

So, I determined that I could buy seven duplexes with the equity left after paying off my existing mortgages at the time of sale. The new seven duplexes would return $332 per unit times 14 units. As an investor, what was I thinking at the time? I knew I needed to do it. The other duplexes in the area were still affordable and represented an extreme change in my cash flow position. Of course, the tricky part was completing it correctly, so the IRS didn't claim most of the cash left in my property.

For those of you who are new to tax law, 1031 Exchanges have rules you MUST follow. If you break the laws, you risk the Exchange causing you to pay all taxes plus penalties. Rather than teach you here in detail, when you're ready for technique in your investment life, enlist someone experienced to guide you flawlessly.

But I can't tell you how many times I hear people say, in an Exchange, you take your property, and you have to find someone else to trade/exchange property. NO, NO, NO! It's way easier than this.

What does this easier way look like? You simply sell your property and insert the clause, "This sale is subject to a 1031 Exchange for the Seller," and both buyer and seller sign. Next, you hire a qualified intermediary. Personally, I hired Starker Services in California, and James is my guy. For those of you looking into 1031 Exchanges, I'm always happy to provide you with his number. As a company, Starker is the original one that challenged the IRS and got the rules more clearly established. And they are helpful and incredibly knowledgeable. Whatever company you chose, use a large, highly-rated group, not a small office. After all, they'll be holding your money until the closing on the properties you buy to replace your original purchase.

To keep this simple... the intermediary signs for you and the money left after paying off the mortgage and closing costs is sent to the intermediary to hold until you purchase new property. They'll sign at closing for you to buy and wire the money necessary to the closing table for you.

After that point, you have 45 days from the closing of the property you're selling to identify the new one or multiple properties. Then you have 180 days from the sale of your property to own the new one or ones. You cannot touch any of the cash, you must use it all, and you must have the same amount or more of mortgage you had on your original property. This is called a "Forward Exchange."

There's also a Reverse Exchange. And what you need to know here is that a Reverse Exchange is done when you buy the property you want first through the intermediary and then sell the other property. This is more complex and a little more expensive.

The costs of doing an Exchange are minimal compared to paying the IRS tens of thousands of dollars. Many are confused and think the amount they pay tax on is the cash they receive. Nothing is further from the truth. You pay tax on your adjusted basis on the property. I track my adjusted basis each year on my spreadsheet with my accountant. And you absolutely can't make a decision about a property unless you know this information. At times, I sell and pay the tax depending on my total tax situation. At other times, I complete a 1031 Exchange.

Frequently Asked Questions

Q: I've heard that rules around taxes are always changing. What's the best way to stay on top of these changes if they're so frequent?

A: Become friends with your accountant. I'm serious! They are an outstanding resource for understanding the ins and outs of what's happening in the tax world, and a good one is always happy to talk about what might work best for your situation.

Q: What's one of the most important factors to understand about 1031 Exchanges?

A: Whatever you do, don't miss your deadlines. Doing so can disqualify all your efforts.

Q: Can I use a 1031 Exchange for my vacation home?

A: This is an excellent question, and because I've worked in markets with strong vacation home rentals, I'm familiar with this topic as well. However, for vacation homes, it can be more difficult to identify if it's an investment property. For this reason, I suggest talking with a professional to ensure your journey to financial freedom is as smooth as possible.

Insider's Tip

I can't recommend enough that you take a tax class. While you'll work hand-in-hand with professionals when it comes to your taxes, you want to have a solid understanding of what's involved. Plus, the classes often provide insight into the nitty gritty aspects of how our tax system works, generally speaking.

CHAPTER 13

PROPERTY MANAGEMENT

This chapter delves into more detail on the specifics involved with property management. In it, we'll go beyond merely having a few tenants to seeing how this service can act as another piece in your journey to financial freedom.

In this chapter, you'll learn about:
- Recognizing the best investments for your dollar
- How to better cater to your tenants
- When to raise your rents for greater value
- Transitioning to a dedicated service

You'll remember from our previous chapters that I would eventually hire a professional property manager and create my own management company. However, it would be something I would personally return to again in the future, and I did develop extensive experience in self-managing over the years. Recall, as well, how you'll need to have an understanding of professional fields like these even if you don't want to long-term manage properties yourself. After all, when you know the ins and outs, you'll be more confident in choosing your own property management company.

As your portfolio of properties and investments grows, you'll be managing more and more tenants. We saw earlier how understanding them can safeguard your investment, but really, how do you understand them better? And if you're talking to them face-to-face, how do you stay objective and tough during the process? You might also be wondering how difficult or easy it is to find tenants to fill 10, 20, or even 100 properties.

Just like every financial situation is a little bit different, every tenant is also different. You probably don't have a difficult time understanding why that is though. From Kentucky to Colorado and New York to Nevada, people are from an unimaginable number of backgrounds. Their personalities have also been shaped by a wide array of personal experiences.

When you meet with them, ask them questions. That's it, but it's a huge part of it all! And listen, *truly* listen to what they have to say. Just like you evaluate your financial situation, you want to evaluate your tenants, but not just for their trustworthiness, also for their needs and their wants.

In order to own and make decisions about a property, you first need to understand who your prospective tenants might be. Create an avatar for them, so you know to what extent you need to improve or maintain your property. For example: Does your likely tenant have children? What ages? Do they work? Are they on welfare? Is your tenant retired? Working class? What income level do you expect? One person or more? Do many of your tenants love to stay in after a long day's work or do they like area amenities?

Different prices and amenities appeal to different people. If your home is low priced and likely to have an abundance of people living in it, carefully evaluate whether you should rehab everything before they move in or if can you improve and make it nice and comparable to other rentals in the area. On that note, try and save the full rehab until just prior to the sale. Recall, this is what I did on Dale Street. The tenants had nice workable kitchens for the ten years leading up to the sale, kitchens which were comparable to other rental properties at that price range at the time. If I had put the new kitchens and baths in Dale St. to begin with, I wouldn't have received any more rent. In addition, the kitchen wouldn't have been bright and new at the time of sale, realizing less profit for me or costing me additional cash to brighten it again.

Consider adding a "wow" feature to your rentals. A "wow" feature is something the tenant who normally rents your home doesn't usually get in a rental. Consider a feature that costs you very little, but in return, helps attract new renters fast and at your top rental rate. Prospective tenants react fast and compete for your property because it's unique. For example, it could be an interesting light or ceiling fan, perhaps a wine cooler, solid surface counters not common in low income rentals, or some plants outside the front walkway. Think simple and special.

In the early days, I simply added a light color to the walls, though not white, and then painted the baseboards white. Two colors of paint make a unit look like a home, and if the tenants felt like it was their home, they would stay longer and take better care of the property. All other rentals were splashed white on everything, making it look cheap and attract less desirable tenants. Today, we add crown molding and wide baseboards with the two-color paint. In these circumstances, it may make total sense to put money into the project, because you know how you'll get your cash back... through increased rental rates.

When initially selecting the right investment property, I look carefully for features that I can uncover or add easily to bring "wow" to my investment. How can you make your property a special place for someone to call "home?"

Buy one with potential.

Truthfully, even different prices appeal to different people. Although you'll want to ensure you don't run afoul of fair housing laws, there is absolutely nothing wrong with understanding everyone who might be interested in your property. By doing so, you can recognize which upgrades command more value, and through additional value, increase your monthly cash.

But you don't have to worry, because you can get individualized advice on the properties you're looking at. Visit my site, book a one-on-one session, and let's talk! Use this link below for your investment coaching session:

http://www.TerryandJason.com/Apply

A word on Fair Housing. Beware! You must not discriminate in any way, shape, or form regarding protected classes. If you do, you could easily be sued and lose everything you've worked your entire life to obtain. Just don't do it.

Be careful and use the same criteria to evaluate tenants every single time. When evaluating tenants, put each one through the same criteria and be sure to keep records. For my journey, I created my own evaluation form with a point system. I included a 140-point system where they earned points based on the following criteria: credit score, job, income, pets, criminal history, unlawful detainer, whether the info they provided was accurate and true, landlord reference, personal references, and even a home visit.

Most people say, "what do you mean home visit?"

I found that I can decide within five seconds of walking into a home whether a tenant takes care of a property or abuses the property. Is there thick grease on the stove? Is the trash stinky and begging to be taken out? Do they take their shoes off? Are there fingerprints everywhere? Even if you give a tenant who doesn't take care of a property a week to prepare, you'll still be able to tell if they take care of the home by doing a simple inspection.

Now, if the tenant wouldn't allow me in, they didn't receive the points, therefore failing to meet the points required to be an acceptable tenant. In retrospect, there was probably a reason they didn't let me in. I can also tell the difference between landlord neglect and tenant neglect, and chances are, so can you. Look carefully! I would also have tenants describe to me, on a scale of one to ten, how they rated themselves on cleanliness. I loved those that said eight, and when I viewed the home, you could eat off the floor! Those were my best tenants.

Now, just because you get to know your tenants, doesn't mean you can't be tough. And if you can't be direct and maintain your expectations, I recommend getting some distance. This fact is especially true if you find yourself being a little overly attached to your units when you start.

Because your tenants will be living in your properties, there will be normal wear and tear, which can be challenging for some new investors to see.

If that's the case, I would definitely recommend a property management company. Even if you're an experienced investor, the extra distance can free you up to focus where you need to: on generating more wealth.

At the same time, there's two factors to keep in mind. First, keep your long and short-term goals in mind at all times, and second, work with professionals who specialize in what you're trying to accomplish. This way, together you should be able to identify specifics on what makes the most sense for each of your investments. From my experience, there are numerous small changes you can make when you acquire a new property, and each one will allow the investment to command greater rents and a better return. There are many improvements you can make that are totally a waste of money. Don't follow your heart renovating the way you would love when it comes to fixing that property. Be objective and purposeful and make good business decisions. Feel free to get other opinions too. If you make the wrong move, it could keep you from achieving your goals in the best way possible. Remember my client earlier who told me that he had purchased "flips," and I told him that he had bought "rentals," not "flips?" His goal was to be a full-time investor. Today, he has a job and is still dealing with his original "flip" properties, which became long term "rentals."

Frequently Asked Questions

Q: If you aren't yet going to hire a property management company, how do you stay objective when dealing with so many people?

A: The best strategy is to create an "Applicant Checklist and Rating System." As I said before, rate everyone equally and hold the line. Do not discriminate; be objective. Establish your criteria; for example: three times the amount of verifiable income to rent, no unlawful detainers, no evictions, no felonies, any credit scores between 525-650 require last month's rent, or no credit score under the number you want it to be.

Q: How much should you spend on upgrades in any given year?

A: You need to evaluate your property annually. What is the current value? What are the current rents? What is my short and long-term plan for the property? What improvements need to be done for my long-term plan? Is it a good time? Will an upgrade improve rents? Will the improvement I make be devalued by the tenant? Or should I wait to rehab later?

For one recent client, I had him add a pool. The home was on a lake in Cape Coral, Florida, and we could obtain $300 more in rent each month once the pool was added. In addition, when he's ready to sell, the pool will return him more than his initial investment. Rather than wait until the pool was complete, I rented the home for $1,595 and raised rent to $1,895 upon completion, stating these terms in the initial lease. This saved my owner valuable downtime later when he would likely be sitting with a vacant home for three months during build time. In addition, we could work on maturing the vegetation in the meantime.

Q: When you hire a property management company, what factors should you look at?

A: A track record of success. Property management isn't a task to take lightly, and you don't want to hire someone who's reputation doesn't precede them. If they don't return calls in a timely manner or can't get someone out to a property quickly, you know that they might not be the right company for you. Do they work weekends? If not, it will take longer to rent your property. This is because most people work during the week.

Is the company proactive in filling your vacancies? Do they treat your property as their own? Do they walk through the home at regular intervals? How do they attract clients? Do they manage other properties like yours? If not, it will be harder. Are they in the area? You want someone who, upon receiving a call from a potentially great tenant, will immediately meet the tenant. Great tenants disappear fast. How long does it take for them to make a decision about a tenant? I can process a tenant in a couple hours. If the company takes days, those good tenants will find another property. How does the company resolve problems? Does their management of your property make your property worth more or less?

For example, I am presently managing a 14-unit building for a gentleman in Fort Myers, Florida. He recently purchased it for just under $1M. Instead of maintaining the status quo, I recommended a few improvements: wide baseboards, crown molding in the living rooms, two colors of fresh paint with exterior paint in a fresh beachy look, and also a picnic area with shade sails and bike racks. I am obtaining $300 more per unit each month. When this project is complete, his investment will double in value, as 14-unit building values are determined by the rents you receive. That is the kind of proactive manager you want managing your asset!

Insider's Tip

Full-time property management can be a challenging piece to your vision, but don't let the difficulties involved weigh you down. Like with any other part of your plan, you'll want to keep the end-goal in mind and take your journey step-by-step. If you love it, you can stick with it; if you don't, you'll soon be able to bring in the pros.

CHAPTER 14
ONE CALL CHANGED
MY LIFE FOREVER

In this chapter, you'll learn how even the most seemingly random encounters can open up entire worlds of opportunity for you... when you're looking out for these encounters. Through these, you can also see how others are equally as enthusiastic as you are about attaining financial freedom.

In this chapter, you'll learn about:

- Recognizing the motivations of others around you
- Maintaining your positive attitude in the face of adversity
- Knowing when to place your highest trust in someone
- Understanding how rare truly driven people are

T he phone was ringing.

It was around 1996, and the market was just starting a healing period, also known as the "absorption" phase of Market Timing. It's characterized in the market as a time when there is a lowering inventory of homes, purchases are picking up, the economy is improving ever slowly, and investors are still hesitant to buy real estate. At the time, I had a triplex listed in a low-income neighborhood for one of my sellers. This property was on the market for $73,900, and I had been hired by a seller to come in and get the job done.

In retrospect, if I had missed this specific call that day, my life might have ended up very differently. Here's why...

The road to financial freedom can be full of its own, very special challenges and rewards. Truthfully, it also comes with its own set of experiences that can be difficult to convey the importance of to others. This fact is certainly true when it comes to friends or co-workers who might not have any interest in generating wealth. Although you'll place your trust in property managers, contractors, CPAs, and many other professionals, they're invested in only a certain part of your vision.

Back to our phone call...

As a real estate agent, I knew, when the phone rang, opportunity may be knocking. So, within a couple short rings, I was on the line, ready to sell that property for my client. However, I would discover so much more than I had ever bargained for.

On the other end of the conversation was Mark Iverson. And what started out as a conversation like any other for a real estate agent became something entirely different. You see, Mark had been listening to Carleton Sheets Seminars. If you've never heard of Carleton Sheets, this was a coaching program that people today pay tens of thousands of dollars for. Sheets was constantly on the TV talking about how rich you could be buying houses. What he neglected to mention, unlike this book, was all the other details that are involved in the process and how to put it into play in everyday life. That's where I fit in.

But Mark was unimaginably hyped on real estate. He didn't want to just buy a triplex, he wanted to make as much money as he could in the process.

Sounds a little familiar, doesn't it?

I could tell right from the start that something was different about Mark and his partner, John. So, I agreed to meet them. From this one phone call, I was about to sit down with two individuals who I would form a lifelong friendship with. In fact, they're the reason I'm here today.

When I showed them what I was doing, their eyes lit up. Instead of just promising riches, I was showing them exactly how to attain those riches, step-by-step. In reality, I was doing what they dreamed of doing. And at the time, I only owned about 14 rental units. Remember, during this period, no one else was really teaching these investment concepts. While the industry was full of get-rich-quick salespeople, there was a serious lack of professionals sharing how to get it done.

Mark and John immediately wanted to know all the details. After listening to those seminars, they were more than eager to learn the specifics. And their enthusiasm completely floored me. It was so contagious, and after working more-or-less on my own to attain financial freedom over the years, I welcomed the conviction and their intensity. And they didn't even know all the real possibilities yet!

So, I sat down with them and taught them what I had learned.

And then I sold them the triplex. They started by using the cash from a credit card, creativity on my part for a principal residence.

Then I sold them a few more properties. Their goals were to quit their day jobs and be full-time investors, creating wealth and attaining financial freedom.

But the story is so much deeper than just a handful of properties being bought or sold. Mark and John are still with me to this very day. As we'll see in our next chapter, they would go on to serve a pivotal role in our story. And beyond the hard numbers or the market cycles we were talking about, there was that hint of more. In these two individuals, I was able to almost immediately sense that their motivations were similar to mine; not in the now-forgotten promises of Carleton Sheets, but in the desire to connect the dots on your own, to develop a system, and to see what extraordinary possibilities lay just beyond the horizon.

This difference wasn't just apparent from the start either. Ever the investor who is evaluating, I started to ask myself questions about what these two were capable of and how our visions overlapped. In fact, I knew that there was a good chance they would be worthy of my highest trust in the business and investing world.

In my experience, a trust built on a shared vision of where you're going and how you should get there can rival even the biggest competitors. At the same time, those partnerships can lift you up in the face of any challenges and in a way that is definitely rewarding, even as it increases your momentum. In the next chapter, we'll see just how true that benefit really is.

Frequently Asked Questions

Q: How specifically did you know so soon that Mark and John might be worthy of your highest trust? Was it just their attitude or was there more?

A: In our next chapter, we're going to talk a bit about how you can recognize the energy someone brings to the table. But the bottom-line is that it's a combination of their positive energy and their will to make things happen, even in the face of obstacles or naysayers. By simply showing up, being open to coaching, eager to learn, willing to take educated risk, and take action when warranted, Mark and John earned my trust, respect, and time. They've even earned the title of "my best clients" to this day.

Q: When I meet other investors, are they evaluating my values and my drive too?

A: Yes! In our day and age, this fact may seem a little intimidating or at odds with what we're taught. However, in the business and investing world, you must be ever-analyzing who's on the same path you're on.

Q: How can I make a better impression on the possible future business partners I meet?

A: My best advice is just to be yourself. That tip may sound simple, but when forming partnerships, it can be crucial to have a clear understanding of each other's strengthens and weakness. More importantly, what are everyone's goals?

Insider's Tip

As you can see, recognizing value, even during everyday interactions, can help build on your vision. Never skip that phone call, ignore that email, or forget to follow up with a friend you ran into at lunch. Although many won't pan out, these seemingly small events contain just as many possibilities as the boardroom meetings or networking events, sometimes more.

CHAPTER 15

ACCELERATE BY SURROUNDING YOURSELF WITH LIKE-MINDED, GOAL-ORIENTED PEOPLE

For this chapter, we'll focus in on how like-minded people can make all the difference in taking your vision to the next level. With them, you'll find you can partner up in a way that benefits all visions involved.

In this chapter, you'll learn about:
- Better utilizing the energy around you
- The payoff when including your most trusted allies in your vision
- The way visions can merge and grow together in complementary ways
- How the results you can achieve can be greater than you ever imagined

How do you know who's legitimately worthy of your trust? And why are allies so important when it comes to your journey to wealth creation?

Let's start with the reasons why discovering these peers is vital and how they differ from members of your team, who you may trust a great deal but with caveats. After all, as an investor, you're more than simply a savvy decision-maker, a real estate agent, or even an employer of people. In reality, you're a leader who will often be called upon to make difficult decisions, to truly understand your market, and sometimes, to let people go from your team.

The truth is that wealth creation is liberating on a level that can be difficult to imagine, let alone explain in detail. While your team members share in that experience, you choose them to tackle the areas they excel at. This means that they may be highly-effective at one piece of the puzzle but only be interested in that piece.

Over time, as you grow your vision, you need allies who understand that journey, and who you can bounce ideas with while keeping the big picture in mind. This means that you're gaining access to a like-minded person who shares in your vision of financial freedom. At the same time, they can also open the doors to a trusted source for information, contacts, and more.

Sounds pretty good, right? And that's only half the story.

Once you've met someone who shares your enthusiasm, ambition, and trust, you're also securing an individual who you can trust with the most intimate details of your enterprise. In some cases, that means taking on a less experienced investor to act as their mentor. In other cases, it serves as a powerful alliance to pave the way to even bigger and better investment activity.

So, how can you recognize this type of person?

For me, there is one fundamental aspect to determining whether someone is worthy of being called your most trusted ally. And that starting place is the energy they give off to those around them, the measure of their own vision in action.

This factor isn't the total story, but it serves as a strong starting point for assessing anyone you meet. And it's as much true whether you're talking to a brand-new real estate agent who's spotted a trend or a boardroom executive with a master plan and decades of experience.

But what does determining someone's energy look like? How do you tell one person's energy apart from another person's?

Placing your trust in others is equal parts based in psychology and an assessment of their process and potential. For wealth creation, these elements come together in a complementary way, one which defines personalities, as well as successes. And when this happens, that person gives off an intensity and a spirit that keys you into their motivations and values.

You can also spot them a mile away.

Let's turn back to my interaction with Mark and John to see how this works. From the moment I began talking with these two, their energy was apparent. They weren't simply enthusiastic about what they were doing, though that was one indicator. In reality, they had a vision they were working toward, and they were on the hunt for a process that works as well.

They just hadn't dreamed big enough yet.

While we would go on to form stronger methods together, Mark and John were willing to ask the difficult questions. Additionally, they treated the people around them in a specific way. For example, they were willing to challenge people around them to go for more, empowering these individuals to even greater things. They also weren't afraid to learn the ins and outs of a subject or to challenge themselves. At the same time, they valued frank conversation, kept their word, and surrounded themselves by others who did too.

You probably know that if you compare any two people, you'll find that they may choose to trust different people, even as they themselves might by worthy of different levels of trust. You may also have noticed in your life how those around you sometimes put their trust in people you might not put your own trust in. You might also have taken note that many people seem to trust or fall out of trust for seemingly the most random reasons. And that's fine, at least for them.

But for you, you'll need a more deep-rooted way of estimating who is reliable enough, honest enough, and determined enough to warrant your trust. Gaining financial independence is a unique combination of choices, who you surround yourself by, and the standards you set for them and yourself. All of these are a big part of your energy.

As an investor, you want to—no, you *must*— hold yourself to a higher standard when it comes to who's around you. In fact, as you enter the investing world, you'll find that countless people will demand your time and energy.

You've probably started to guess that your energy matters too. And others are checking to see how it measures up.

It's impossible to overstate the power of a positive "can-do" attitude. The investing world is full of challenges that can wear down the best of us at times. There's nothing more powerful and motivating than being around others doing the same thing and when their energy is positive and fun.

Frequently Asked Questions

Q: How do you avoid getting burnt by someone you might have thought you could trust at first?

A: This is an excellent question, especially because many of people who are starting their journey to financial freedom may have experienced being burnt once or twice in their past. My biggest tip is not to give someone new the keys to your kingdom right off the bat. Instead, slowly increase their responsibilities and your level of trust as they prove themselves. This fundamental idea—that trust is earned, not given by accident—is vital. The old saying is correct though, if they burn you once, don't let them burn you twice! Trust your intuition. Get out and cost losses immediately.

Q: How can you better align your own energy for those people around you?

A: This is another question I'm asked frequently, and I love it, because it shows you're thinking about your impact on others. In reality, as you attain financial freedom, you're often touching the lives of countless people with every decision you make. I've always found that if you seek to do right by others, even when it's difficult to do so, they'll do the same to you, and that can mean all the difference. Serve those who deserve your attention and add to your energy field. Be wary of those who drain you. I make the mistake of trying to help negative people, often soon realizing they choose their perspective, and it won't change unless they want it to change.

A word on family: be careful. I've encountered many clients whose parents or siblings were negative on their investment endeavor. If so, just don't share with them. My father is very proud of me; however, sometimes all my transactions cause him undue stress. I found it is better to share with people who share your energy and your goals. My late mother, Peggy Records, in the last decade of her life, embraced real estate and rentals. She and I even obtained our real estate licenses at the same time. And she and I breathed real estate together. Even though she worked in Florida and I worked in Minnesota, we shared all we knew with each other. My siblings, Stephen and Tricia, to this day, still complain of how boring Mom and I were at that time period because we were obsessed with learning our new endeavor. But we didn't care, because we were having fun building wealth and learning together.

Q: Were you able to identify Mark and John as allies from the very start or did it take time?

A: From the moment I met them, I knew that something was different. Sure, I had worked with some outstanding clients. But this was vastly more unique when I met Mark and John, from the very beginning. We started with the first deal and as their knowledge base grew, they began to contribute more to the big picture. Instead of just using my energy and knowledge, they began to contribute with their energy, seeking to fill gaps with additional contractors, potential lenders, and another viewpoint when evaluating neighborhoods and potential properties.

Wondering how to find strong allies or strengthen the relationships with your current allies? Visit my site, and let's talk about it! You can book a one-on-one investment coaching session with the link below:

http://www.TerryandJason.com/Apply

Insider's Tip

Now, it's important to keep in mind that your life doesn't have to be mirror image of your allies' lives. Consider how Mark was and still is passionate about dirt track racing. While it's not my interest, I can appreciate that he has that catalyst in his life. By becoming wealthy with real estate, he was able to afford the one-ton pickup truck to haul his modified and late-model race cars, and later, a home in Florida on a gulf-access canal with a boat of his dreams. I still remember the first day I went to the race track with him: it was Mother's Day and I thought, "really?" Not on my bucket list for Mother's Day! I later learned to use my time at the track to unwind and rejuvenate, and much later, spent dozens of weekends enjoying my time there.

CHAPTER 16
MY FUTURE HUSBAND, JASON

To get even more of a sense how all these factors can come together at once, we'll pivot back to how my personal story grew in an unexpected way and with a surprising new ally. Through this surprising change, I would be able to look toward my first million.

In this chapter, you'll learn about:

- The desire for financial freedom existing in people from all walks of life
- How even with the scarcest of resources, you can attain financial freedom
- The way all your planning can make a difference in one person's vision
- The impact of your energy and how it feeds back into your personal life

But something else would come from that initial phone call with Mark, and it was something that was completely unpredictable. And yet, it was completely a product of my own energy and my own vision. As we'll soon see, it also propelled me to a level of financial success most people only dream about.

After selling a few properties to Mark and John, my life started to take a new turn. Remember, up until this point, I was largely pursuing my vision on my own. Sure, there were plenty of people involved in that vision, from plumbers to tenants and mortgage lenders to property inspectors. But when it came to financial freedom, I was the one juggling all the different priorities and challenges. I also realized that I could impact other investors and began pursuing that journey, helping these investors build wealth by selling real estate.

The more that Mark and John proved themselves, the more trust I placed in them. And from that unity, we were increasingly becoming more efficient in our investing and more driven to accomplish bigger goals. For example, as I look back, technically we were all inexperienced investors in those days. For example, we were very eager to learn, but we had no model to follow or coach to instruct us. So, we teamed together and looked at hundreds and hundreds of properties.

While in constant discussion, we ended up fine-tuning and created our own real estate investment model. Once we were in agreement about what we were looking for, it made it easy to make an immediate decision to purchase property or whether the tenant was suitable to fill our vacancy. Even though we were technically in competition with each other, we never actually were. One of the reasons this is true is because I believe on operating in abundance. There are enough deals out there for everyone. And not everyone is prepared to make a decision every day of the week. The person who is preapproved with cash in hand is the one who gets to make the offer that day. I apply the same principle to all my clients every day and rarely do any of my investors compete with one another.

We continued to look at more properties and learned the ins and outs of other neighborhoods. But we also strategized, reviewed the data, and challenged each other's assumptions. Financial freedom became our passion and our promise to each other. We would maximize on each other's energy to see just what we were capable of together.

Now, imagine for a moment if you saw this situation from the outside.

For the common investor or real estate agent, they would see a tremendous level of activity that can be hard to match or compete against alone. For someone else, say a working-class person with dreams of getting out of the rat race, they would see an impressive avenue toward finding wealth.

That fact was true for at least one individual, a carpenter named Jason Nordhougen. Now, Jason was a hard-working person with two jobs, one part-time and involving contracting work like building cabinetry for kitchens and woodworking; the other, a full-time job driving a semi-truck. He was, by all appearances, a regular guy with a sweet smile and an exceptional work ethic. He had recently moved to Minnesota to be nearby his 12-yr. old daughter, Joslyn.

And because of Jason's attention to factors like craftsmanship and detail, Mark had brought Jason in to help renovate properties. Working on their properties began to make Jason think and evaluate what was happening around him. For him, he wasn't happy with the status quo now. At the time, Mark had helped Jason get employed at Old Dutch, where Mark worked when Jason moved to town. Now, Jason and Mark were doing the same "job," but Mark was driving the nice truck and racing modified race cars, while Jason drove a 225,000-mile Datsun pickup. What was missing? After a couple weekends of working on their properties, he asked them. Mark and John explained what we were doing and talked about how their real estate agent, Terry, was helping them accomplish their goals.

In reality, Jason, like any ordinary American, was recently divorced and had experienced his own fair share of credit issues. He was also short on cash. In fact, he had just financed his Datsun at a whopping 26% interest rate, because, of course, he needed a truck to get to work, and he had to work.

So, after another agent and mortgage broker told Jason that he couldn't buy a house, Mark brought him to me.

From there, I met with Jason in my office and asked him about his goals for the future. He told me he didn't really enjoy his job and would like to own properties himself, homes he could work on. And he also wanted to quit his job. It was also apparent that the love for his daughter was paramount. He had left a job he loved as a cabinet maker in another state to follow her to Minnesota. And there, he was working a job, one which left him feeling unfulfilled.

And the problem he had was that he had no cash and poor credit. Sound familiar?

I talked to him about the basics of investing, and somehow, we got lost in our conversation about a mutual desire for being in a place called Montana. Here was this down-to-earth guy, who was from a modest background, and the entire time, he's trying to find a way to do what he does best for other people.

And to attain his own financial freedom.

Now, I told him not to up and quit his job that day. He would need to meet a few financial goals first. However, I told him I could help him achieve those goals if he applied a few simple steps that I would help identify for him. I was touched by his demeanor, humility, and respect.

Okay, okay, *okay*... he was good looking too! Our first meeting ended with my one-of-a kind handshake, where you use both hands to shake both sides of the other person's hand. I haven't used that handshake for anyone else since.

I took this as a sign.

If you'll recall from our initial chapters, our next step would be strategically purchasing a principal residence. And that's exactly what I helped Jason do. First, we found a loan officer with a can-do attitude, one willing to work with him. Doreen Drake, my ace loan officer, entered his life, and instead of denying him for a loan, gave him a loan at 12.9% for his first purchase at 1017 Englewood in St. Paul.

Now, many might say, "No, I want 8.9%, and I'll wait until my score is high enough."

Instead, I told Jason how, by acting now, he could buy a home at a lower price and improve the home, making it worth more money. He would only have 12.9% rate temporarily, and once the rehab was done, he could refinance at a lower rate, because his credit would have more time to heal. It was also a factor in this equation to help him to replenish his seed corn. Refinancing did cost some cash in closing costs, but the interest rate was lower. He took out $15,000 cash, and his payment stayed the same.

Before you knew it, Jason and I were dating. I'll admit that there was a lot to like about him. Just to be clear, I didn't kiss him until after he wrote his first purchase agreement. And when that happened, it was lightly snowing one night in the parking lot at my office at 821 Grand Avenue. Of course, I remember the night clearly; after all, it's hard to forget after such an unexpected event. You see, after dinner and a kiss from Jason, my elderly neighbor, Jim, and I rescued a plump Labrador from an icy, frozen river behind my home on Grey Cloud Island. Much to my chagrin, emergency services wouldn't rescue dogs, or so we discovered when we called 911.

The point being that I associated that Labrador we saved with Jason's love for his daughter, Joslyn, who also had a Labrador named Molly. In a roundabout way, it was an omen.

But Jason's knowledge of historic craftsmanship was impressive, and his desire to help others made him stand out. Jason would tell you the thing that impressed him most about me was that I drove a nice, newer suburban with leather seats. However, it wasn't actually the nice truck I drove, but the fact I would put my 125lb golden retriever, Kody, in it and drive around town. Now, by this point, Jason had already told me about his daughter and the love they had for their late lab, Molly. Little did he know, I had simply brought Kody to bring joy to Joslyn while we were out on showings. Still, Jason was also levelheaded, plainspoken, and driven, all qualities that let me know, when he committed to something, there was no stopping him.

In fact, it wasn't long before we found him a few more additional properties!

For Jason, the journey of financial freedom was just beginning; for both us, the road to a loving partnership was already in full swing.

Of course, from Jason's perspective, he also saw that Mark, John, and I were having a blast. And I mean an absolutely amazing time. It might be hard to believe at first, but we were so wrapped up in understanding our market and making money that we were loving every single second of it. In fact, one Sunday, as we all looked at a duplex on Ottawa over on the Westside, the tenants were shouting and cheering next to us in the living room, and we found ourselves wondering what all the excitement could be about.

It was Super Bowl Sunday. Can you believe it?

We were feeding off each other's energy so much and loving what we were doing to the point that we had completely forgotten about this major sporting event. So, you can imagine how Jason, who was at the edges of all this intensity, was feeling.

Frequently Asked Questions

Q: Is it really possible for anyone to achieve financial freedom in today's day and age?

A: I wanted to address this question at this point in our story for a specific reason. As you can see, Jason was your average guy, devoted to what he loved and from humble beginnings. Mark and John were also just regular individuals. Of course, I don't at all want to downplay who they are as people, but along with my own story, you can see that we weren't millionaires to start off.

Q: How important is it in business to make time for family and even love?

A: Without question, you have to make time for yourself. Investing and financial freedom can give you unspeakable liberty, and I've loved every second of it. But by making time for those you love most, you're ensuring that you step away from the numbers and the deals to see why it all matters so much.

Q: When can I quit my job on my journey to financial freedom?

A: We'll see in our next chapter exactly when Jason decided to quit his job, but for now, my advice is to look at your cash flow. The sweet spot is 150% monthly cash flow above all your normal living expenses, so you can still budget money for factors like repairs.

Over the years, I've mentored countless real estate agents and investors on finding that sweet spot. When you have questions about attaining that 150% monthly cash flow and your unique situation, visit my site. You can schedule an individualized session with me, so we can talk about what's right for you:

http://www.TerryandJason.com/Apply

Insider's Tip

When it comes to obtaining financial freedom, if you're short on assets, it may not seem like it, but cash is one of the easiest resources to generate as a first step. Whether you're working extra hours to reduce debt and get access to more credit or putting a down payment on your principal residence, these often involve having a small amount of cash in hand, which requires nothing more than a little extra hard work.

CHAPTER 17
THE FIRST MILLION:
MARCH 6TH, 1999

In more than one way, this chapter represents an important milestone in my personal story to attain financial freedom. Reaching your first million is an accomplishment you'll remember for the rest of your life, and there's a few financial lessons to be learned from my personal experience. Still, the day I attained it was extra special for me.

In this chapter, you'll learn about:

- Pooling assets and resources with liked-minded people to generate extraordinary changes in your circumstances
- The fruition of one of the strongest alliances you can make
- Balancing your allies out in productive ways to attain your vision
- The thrill of quitting your day job for financial independence

F rom outside, the Minnesota sky, though brisk, seemed to threaten yet another snow storm, much to the chagrin of my mother, who was from Florida. It was one of those beautiful days you have a hard time forgetting, even if you want to. From inside, the bed and breakfast was a cozy mix of western style and rustic décor, and all our friends and family had arrived there to be with us.

I was about to marry Jason and hit $1,000,000, all at the same time.

On my road to financial freedom, if you recall, there had been several moments when I wished I had dreamed even bigger. And for many people, the idea of attaining a net worth of a million dollars can seem like a far-off fantasy, something to daydream about when you have down time.

At this point in my journey, however, as I stood across from Jason, I was beginning to realize something. And that was how financial freedom and wealth creation weren't just about money. Sure, the capital was part of it. But in reality, my decisions had put me on a path toward meeting people who shared my goals. It would also take me from my seemingly everyday life as a real estate agent to the extraordinary point of securing $1,000,000 in assets. That's quite a change!

And I was seeing now that it was truly only the spark of all that could be possible.

But let's back up a little bit, and see how this day, my wedding day and just one day before my birthday, had come to be. It wasn't by accident that I would be worth a million dollars with the stroke of a pen.

If you remember from our last chapter, Jason had impressed me with his goals and his values. And after selling him his principal residence, strategically purchased in an edge district that would soon gentrify, he would quickly acquire six more of his own units. After taking stock of his financial resources, he was able to tap a $30,000 private loan from a family member, and within only 6 months, he had leveraged his assets into a remarkable portfolio.

Oh, did I mention? He also quit his job and paid back the original loan.

Remember what I said about like-minded people and their energy? Jason was the living proof that earned trust can do remarkable things, and in a far shorter timeframe than I had originally thought possible. You should definitely take note here, because one of the most important things I have to teach you is that you can take my experience and put it on a faster timeline to attain your goals.

Now, I had advised Jason to wait before he quit his job. He needed three more properties under his belt to maximize his cash flow. But as you can imagine, after gaining his 6th unit, he was primed to say "goodbye" to working for someone else. You see, Jason also had a love of dirt track racing, and more than anything, he wanted to spend his time doing what he did best. For him, that was restoring properties, building cabinetry, and spending time with family. The very day he quit his job, his personality became even more energetic about what we were building together, and he was especially proud of all we were doing.

When it comes down to it, while I wouldn't change what I recommended about waiting to quit his job, I admired his passion and willingness. Jason was astonishingly good at outpacing even his own goals, and this was the kind of energy I was talking about earlier. You can truly recognize it when you see it.

By the time we were standing next to each other at that bed and breakfast in Minnesota, I was worth about $850,000 and had my own portfolio of strategically acquired properties. In the meantime, Jason had built a respectable $150,000 foundation of his own out of the $30,000 loan from family. Together, we would pay for all our family and friends to stay at nearby hotels, so they could be part of the magic. Jason had also sold his principal residence to pay for his part of the wedding and move into my home on Grey Cloud Island. He was proud that he had an asset that could help him accomplish his next goal.

Still, alliances like these produce more than simply larger numbers, which sound good on paper. With Jason, I had gained a partner with a track record for meticulous, intelligent decision-making. He was also exceptionally versed in not just adding in new kitchen cabinets or installing light fixtures. In addition, Jason enjoyed his new opportunity to learn and view many different architectural styles and details of different time periods. He also followed the latest in rehab trends and liked to consider exactly which type of upgrades would increase rents and property values. And he was truthful, open, and willing to help others. Finally, he was also inclined to take calculated, well-thought-out risks that aligned with his vision and goals. Truthfully, we complemented each other in ways that made us a force to be reckoned with when it came to wealth creation.

We still maintained a future goal of being in Montana together, and if you know the area, you know how the landscape can often be a handsome testament to the natural world. For me, Montana also represents proof that, when two people's visions overlap, they can achieve goals that reshape their very universe.

Frequently Asked Questions

Q: How difficult was it to find love on your road to find your financial freedom?

A: As long as you surround yourself with like-minded people who have the right energy, you'll have no trouble building relationships that stand the test of time. In my career, I have experienced it firsthand.

Q: Is there a target amount of cash flow you recommend a person have before living off the budget exclusively?

A: So, in our previous chapter, we saw how I recommend 150% cash flow monthly before quitting your job. However, let's take this a step further. To live exclusively off your wealth creation, you must carefully crunch your numbers against your desired lifestyle. This number will differ for every single person, because their monthly expenses may be slightly different. This is why I always recommend pairing with an experienced mentor before taking that big step toward financial freedom.

Q: Do you tell your husband, and in this case, your business partner, everything? Is it important to do so?

A: My answer is "yes." On the road to wealth creation, there are many challenging decisions to make, and if you're leaving your most trusted ally in the dark, how will they provide you with the best of their skills and knowledge? It's important to goal plan together. You may not have the same goals, but if your dream is big enough, it can encompass both sets of goals in a complementary way.

Insider's Tip

From this chapter, you can see how we used the financial resources at our fingertips to have the wedding we wanted. But one of my biggest pieces of advice is that you must balance your financial vision with your personal lifestyle. While you'll need to make sacrifices along the way, you can see how they fit into the bigger picture for the life you want to lead.

CHAPTER 18

THE SECOND MILLION:
THE YEAR 2000

This chapter demonstrates just how quickly your road to financial freedom will accelerate as you get further into your journey. While the initial steps can seem like they're taking forever at first, the jump from $1 million to $2 million can be incredibly rapid.

In this chapter, you'll learn about:

- How to stay focused on your journey by anticipating the rewards
- Advanced methods of analyzing your financial situation
- Relying on your own critical thinking instead of just technology
- How your priorities and definition of fun transforms
- Preventing money from changing who you are

I n the everyday world, many people underestimate just how capital attracts more capital. In a certain sense, we understand the idea when it comes to say, businesses. For example, someone with millions of dollars will have an easier time starting multiple revenue-generating businesses than someone who only has $100,000.

However, the same holds true when it comes to investing and wealth creation in general. A simple example might help illustrate the principle. Say two people buy into a business they believe in by purchasing a company's stock on the stock market. The first person only has a few hundred dollars, while the second has $100,000. If they equally invest all their funds, for every point up the stock moves, the person with the larger sum is accumulating more wealth. What this means is that it's easier to make money when you have money.

How does this apply to our story?

After Jason and I married and began making ventures together, our timeline accelerated to an unimaginable point. Once upon a time and many years before this point, we would have considered it a good year if we did say, 20 solid deals. Many real estate agents will tell you that's respectable. You may even be surprised to find out that, according to some sources, many real estate agents will have less than 10 deals a year.

After we hit $1,000,000, it wasn't uncommon for us to be doing in excess of 10 deals in a single month personally and another 10 for our clients.

You can probably imagine how significant this time felt for us. But the reality is that the number of deals you do isn't what's important, not in and of themselves. Think about it for a moment: if you're churning through properties, but you're also spending all your seed corn on those same properties... what are you really gaining? By all standards, you're probably just getting a lot of hard work for nothing.

At this point, we need to discuss a more advanced method for assessing your financial situation, and that method is your cash-on-cash return.

Cash-on-cash return is the concept of determining your rate of return for a transaction based on the money put in and the money you'll get out. Okay, I'm sure you're thinking that sounds great, but what does it mean in layman's terms? You want to know how much cash you must put up and how much you'll get back to make an opportunity happen.

For those of you with a real estate background, this concept may be familiar to you, but only in a limited sense. Instead of only determining my cash-on-cash return for the first year, as is common in real estate, I was determining it regularly and for every change. Rents went up one month? I re-ran all the numbers. Adding a bathroom or stainless-steel appliances into a property would cause it to command an additional $10,000 at sale? I would re-run all the numbers.

We'll see later why it's so important to be calculating this data beyond your initial transactions, but rest assured that it can give you monumental insight into your position as an investor.

What's the bottom-line? Because the more equity you have changes how quickly you can generate wealth, your cash-on-cash return changes based on your present value, mortgage amounts, and rents. Think back to our stock example: when you own 100 shares of a stock, and it goes up $1.00, you have $100.00. Now, imagine if you owned 1,000 shares of that same stock. Your capital works far faster for you. And through cash-on-cash return, you're able to see how every dollar you're using feeds back into your own wealth.

A real-world example might also help here. At this point, Jason and I owned a set of 20 duplexes. In one year, rents went up and continued to climb. It didn't take long for them to jump from $650 to $850 per month. And while we were paying to maintain these properties, the monthly cash-flow increased. By the end of the year, we were surprised when those values rose by $50,000 per duplex.

Our cash flow had increased on a monthly basis. Pretty easy to understand, and we didn't even have to get bogged down in fancy calculations or complex financial jargon!

Because of the unexpected appreciation of the 20 duplexes, our net worth went from $1,000,000 to $2,000,000 one year just because they increased in value. This was also the time right before 9/11, and although we'll see later how lending practices by the Federal Reserve fueled future changes, the lesson still remains... capital generates more capital, and you must know how yours is working for you.

Two final points before we move onto our next financial concept in the following chapter.

First, whatever you do, don't simply use an app to calculate your cash-on-cash return or any of the other formulas you find most helpful for your financial journey. Even though those apps can be helpful, you as a beginning investor need to understand how cash-on-cash returns work. No one else will do it for you. It is the basis of understanding your investment. You need to be so familiar with making these calculations you can do it in your sleep. This is because you're going to be doing it on-the-fly during transactions and deals, and the last thing you want is to hesitate and need to turn to an app. Decisions on the spot are where a lot of money is made after doing your homework.

Second, and most importantly, your definition of fun really does change at this point. Recall how my business partners and I were so wrapped up in what we were doing that we forgot it was Super Bowl Sunday one day? As you attain this level of financial independence, your priorities refocus. You're so busy running your numbers and tracking every change in your situation, all in service of having your capital work better for you, it becomes something you live and breathe. You must have those critical thinking skills (and if you're reading this book, you're the sort of person that already has an idea of how important this factor can be).

I can confidently say that I don't need an app to run my cash-on-cash. In reality, I barely need a spreadsheet anymore, and I can determine in the flash of an eye whether or not a deal will work to further my financial goals.

Although this skill is exceptionally helpful, you can't lose sight of what's most important to you. Without question, $1,000,000 is a good deal of money for a lot of people. When money is moving hands rapidly throughout your month, it can be tempting to become obsessed with just how hurriedly you can make more money.

On paper, that sounds great. But for your journey to financial freedom, you must be patient, not carelessly hasty; deliberate and intelligent, not rushed or thoughtless. Stay focused on building those skills needed to get yourself to this point and further. We've seen how the rewards can be substantial, from paying all your bills to quitting your day job. Keep those rewards—and your goals—in mind as you enter this stage of your journey. Make sure you stay levelheaded.

Frequently Asked Questions

Q: I've heard stories about lotto winners going bankrupt within years of winning. How do you keep your head on your shoulders after having attained financial freedom and having large amounts of capital?

A: Restocking your seed corn and checking your cash-on-cash return. I'm not joking about how critical these concepts are! Those lotto winners you hear about, flush with millions, run out and spend, spend, spend. But now you know, when you restock your seed corn and determine your cash-on-cash return, you can maintain your wealth, instead of merely spending it all away.

Q: Is cash-on-cash return the only formula I need to know? What other ones are important?

A: When generating wealth, cash-on-cash is by far the most basic to understand. Additionally, appreciation and depreciation play a factor in your situation, as can interest. However, for the initial stages of your journey, you'll want to focus on cash-on-cash return. The total return on investment is also key. Jeff Wirth of the Wirth Companies of Minneapolis said at one seminar I attended long ago, if you can obtain a 30% total return on investment year after year, you will become a billionaire.

Q: What if I still want to do the activities I love even after I attain financial freedom, like watching sports, for example?

A: You can do that! I don't want to suggest that you throw your passions out the window when you attain financial freedom. In fact, the opposite is true. Now, during your leisure time, you're watching the Big Game on your in-home projector with all your friends. If that's important to you, there's no reason it still shouldn't be. But you're also thinking about what opportunities surround sports as well, as we'll see in one of our later chapters.

Insider's Tip

The momentum involved at this stage of financial freedom can mean volatility for many people. Due to human psychology, new investors can continue to take on bigger risks without checking how it works for them. Instead, use your most trusted allies to help check your assumptions and always return to the numbers. Using educated risks is key, and we'll see in the next chapter how that's possible with the concept of market anomalies.

Of course, you always have a trusted ally in me. As you look to increase your wealth, we can talk one-on-one about the risks and rewards that apply to your individual situation. Book an investment coaching session with me to get started:

http://www.TerryandJason.com/Apply

CHAPTER 19

MARKET ANOMALIES

In this chapter, we'll introduce an advanced concept that applies to everything from financial trading to mortgage loans. The idea itself is fairly straightforward, but identifying them, especially in the moment, is one of the most difficult aspects of your road to financial freedom.

In this chapter, you'll learn about:

- Markets all across the world and how they produce anomalies
- The way anyone, with the right mindset, can find anomalies
- The rarity of these situations and how they often end quickly
- Identifying these opportunities in the moment

Let's say you went down to your local store one day, only to discover that they had mismarked a product by a generous amount. To your astonishment, you even discover that the price is so low, you can purchase ten of the items for the price of what one normally would cost.

If you found yourself in that situation, what would you do? How would you act?

Well, if you're like most people, you'd stock up and take advantage of the oversight when you had the chance. Maybe you'd even buy a considerable amount more than you usually would, storing up for a rainy day, as they say. You would probably fully expect that this irregularity would be closed up the moment it was discovered.

And would you be surprised to find out that savvy investors do the exact same thing?

I love it when inexperienced real estate agents underprice properties by tens of thousands; it's like Christmas morning, and one of my most favorite things.

At its heart, our initial situation in this chapter is an anomaly, albeit an uncomplicated one. Yet, across the world, anomalies are being created in the most unlikely of places. From the supermarket down the road to the information superhighway of the Internet, small deviations in the way things are done slip through the cracks without anyone noticing. In many cases, once they're found out, the process is changed, and the anomaly is gone for good.

Why are anomalies so important on your road to wealth generation?

Market anomalies are short-lived opportunities when the window is left open for savvy investors who are ready. These investors are able to identify the opportunity and get busy taking advantage of it before it's gone. Here's your first example:

In 1999-2000, Mark was particularly talented at going to lenders and negotiating favorable deals. And as we saw in our last chapter, rents were on the rise. But equally true, property values were beginning to climb as well.

This wasn't our entire strategy; however, Mark was able to take advantage of the relationships he had established with lenders. Through those connections, he had the ability to get us what today would be known today as a rehab loan. At the time, no one else had heard of it. To keep our story simple: we would ask a local bank to lend us money to buy in a part of town at the edge of where investors were currently interested. Instead of buying the less-than-ideal property for say, $45,000, we would buy it at $57,000 and put a 10% down payment to purchase the home. In addition, we had the homeowner pay $12,000 to our contractor at closing for work that would be completed after closing; essentially, putting $5,700 down while getting $12,000 for repairs. Remember seed corn? We were keeping track of ours. And we completed the work immediately after closing, filled the vacancy in the property, and then waited for the right opportunity in the future.

All of this activity, from loans to rehabs and negotiations to final sale, were fueled by one simple anomaly... those rehab loans, which are far more regulated today than they were at that time. We did them as fast as we could. As soon as we could put together the cash for a down payment, we would buy another property. Again and again.

What I find most amazing about market anomalies is that they can be identified by anyone who's paying attention. You don't need a special degree in economics or advanced training in financial matters. In all honesty, you only need to use what we've been talking about right here in these chapters: your own critical thinking, your willingness to ask questions, and the readiness to know your market like the back of your hand.

A couple years went by, and other investors around us were starting to catch on to what we were doing. That current market situation, which had started to speed up in the years after 9/11, was also in part accelerated by the Federal Reserve. The Fed, as it's often called, had changed their approach, and with new standards and increasing values, came hordes of even more new investors. When they saw what we were doing, they wanted a piece of the action. The demand from the rest of the market, as they caught up to us, caused prices to increase sharply, even though we didn't plan for it. We had bought purely on cash flow, not potential appreciation.

Of course, identifying anomalies in the moment means you need to be paying attention, even while others aren't. That's not always easy, psychologically speaking. But today, other successful investors like Nassim Nicholas Taleb have said exactly what I've been saying since I began my journey to financial freedom.

And they're saying how regular, everyday people like you and me are often able to see what even the academic experts can't.

Your financial freedom is possible through your own ability to spot a good deal and take advantage of it while it's available. Of course, if it were as simple as "buying low and selling high," as they say, anyone could do it. There's much more to it, as you're discovering. But the facts speak for themselves, and it's clear that, when you spot an anomaly, you should pay extra attention.

In the next chapter, we'll look at another example of a market anomaly, and how it helped me to continue building my wealth.

Frequently Asked Questions

Q: The world surrounding investment markets can feel astonishingly complex when I first look at it. Does this get better over time?

A: Yes! You have to remember that it benefits certain types of investors to drown regular people in complicated sounding jargon and formulas. Those terms and calculations have their place, but as you can see, I differ my investing mentorship by stressing how financial freedom is possible for anyone. Like with any other activity, with time, you become more comfortable with the process.

Q: What if I believe that I've seen anomalies in the past, but didn't act on them?

A: They're likely gone. You should still do your research and thoroughly check over them. This can be worthwhile practice until you spot the next one. Don't worry though, because there's always something new. You just have to be looking and in tune with your market. It's not what people are talking about; it's about analyzing your market and foreseeing where the trends are and taking educated action.

Q: Should I always take advantage of every single market anomaly I discover?

A: I would suggest, instead of jumping at any anomaly you find, stop and re-assess how you might incorporate it into your existing position and strategies. Asking how an anomaly can further benefit your vision is the fundamental question to determine before making a decision.

Insider's Tip

There's one big mistake that most new investors make when they start looking for market anomalies. And that's identifying one at its very end. In their excitement, they may not fully determine if the anomaly is still profitable for their situation and jump in. This can often lead to razor-thin cash flows and difficult situations.

CHAPTER 20
THE CASH-OUT REFINANCE

This chapter combines several of the concepts we've been talking about and provides an additional real-world example of market anomalies. You'll also learn how paying attention to factors like your cash-on-cash return can give you insight into making the best decisions for your personal financial situation.

In this chapter, you'll learn about:

- Additional examples taken from actual experience, not textbooks
- Carefully monitoring your existing financial situation to continue momentum
- How small, overlooked anomalies can have big effects
- The difference between letting your wealth grow or shrink
- Setting the stage for branching out into new businesses

B y now, I hope you're appreciating how the details matter. What often appears to be a completely insignificant circumstance to most people can have profound effects. And when you're able to see how your money is working for you, dollar by dollar and property by property, you can build a foundation where almost anything is possible.

In this lesson, we're going to tackle the cash-out refinance, but first, let's look at an indispensable idea that may not be obvious at first glance.

When it comes to your financial situation, no matter how much money you have, your wealth is either growing or shrinking. By no means is it a static number etched in stone. Every day, you're either generating cash flow with the assets and time you possess, or you aren't.

Many people think of wealth as a stopping place, a number they might attain in a checking account before calling it quits. However, the opposite is true. Remember the lotto winners we talked about earlier? They had untold fortunes handed to them, and in the blink of an eye, they shrank them to nothing. Through their attitude, they spent themselves to bankruptcy in more than a few cases.

You're different, however. Above all else, you now understand from my personal journey that wealth is a process of nurturing and growing. That process is constant and on-going. From the moment you start your own journey to financial freedom, you're on the path to develop your wealth, not merely maintain the status quo.

From this philosophy, as basic as it sounds, you can gain insight into your financial momentum. You can also take offensive or defensive positions with your positions to ensure your wealth is preserved over time.

In essence, this fact is why regularly identifying anomalies, however small, and running your cash-on-cash return is so necessary. And we're about to see exactly how that can play out with the cash-out refinance.

To keep our story uncomplicated, let's look at a plain definition of what a cash-out refinance loan looks like.

When you refinance a home, you're taking out another loan beyond your existing mortgage loan. Today, many people are familiar with this type of lending. Now, in a cash-out refinance, the new loan is for a greater amount than the initial mortgage loan. Why would you want a loan bigger than your first one?

In a cash-out refinance, you get the difference between the two loans in cash. There are a few other notable differences, such as the consolidation of debt into one loan and differing interest rates. But for now, you've probably guessed why there's a benefit here.

Cold, hard cash.

Besides the cash, however, there is further benefit you'll love... refinancing is not taxable. And you'll recall from our chapter on taxes how important your tax situation can be.

But where's the anomaly? Excellent question.

In 2001 and 2002, I discovered a fluke that would help grow my wealth to the next level. Around this time, I was immersed in the smallest of details while analyzing our big picture. So, you can imagine my surprise when my strategic lender, Doreen Drake, called and said she had cash-out refinances available at a considerably lower interest rate.

How low are we talking here? Instead of the typically 10.5% interest of the time, I could get cash-out refinancing at 8.5%. However, a solid interest rate was only one aspect of this anomaly. When I asked my lender how many they were willing to do at this rate her answer shocked me.

There was no limit, not at the moment. So, I quickly told her to immediately refinance all my properties. I wanted them all refinanced within a 3-month period. I had identified another anomaly and was going to use it before it went away. They did limit the number to ten about six months later, whew!

Now, in today's market, you can still refinance as many times as you want, but there are other regulations and factors involved, such as changing interest rates, as well as conforming and nonconforming loans. These can make it less desirable in some situations. Yet, here I was with a lender willing to give me a low interest rate for as many loans as I wanted, and I would gain the cash while mitigating my taxes at the same time.

Would it shock you to hear that we did 34 of these loans without hesitation? By doing so, we took out $750,000 in cash at one go. Overall, if you added all our new payments together and compared to our other payments prior to refinancing, our payment went up a mere $150. Now would you take $750,000 and pay $150 more a month? Yes!

Keep in mind that we didn't make this decision in a vacuum. Consider what I said earlier about property values continuing to rise. Rents were increasing, but the spreads between what we were paying and what we were getting were changing. As they did, we were carefully watching our cash-on-cash return, which was beginning to slip down. With this change, we sought to improve those numbers and generate more cash flow.

So, what did we do with that $750,000? Did we spend it all on luxury cars and mansions?

Absolutely not. While we were able to enjoy the lifestyle we wanted, we also funneled that cash back into our financial freedom. We purchased an additional 25 units and renovated our existing homes, from kitchens and roofs to furnaces and landscape. We also improved our existing inventory of properties, so they would command higher rents and sale prices at their eventual sale.

By securing our wealth generation, we were also building a launch point for tacking on additional revenue streams. Through these deals and ones like them, new business ventures were just on the horizon.

Frequently Asked Questions

Q: Why is it so important to focus on real-world examples?
A: For some of my readers, this will be rather obvious. The classroom has its place, and I teach seminars myself. But without real world examples, you're focusing on theory, not practice. We've seen a multitude of times when the experts got it wrong or totally overlooked what was happening. Instead, I focus on experience that has been tested and succeeded.

Q: What happens if you aren't running your cash-on-cash return and miss something?

A: As we'll see in Chapter 22 and 23, 2008 was just such a year for many people. Untold numbers of investors fell asleep at the wheel... and were wiped out, sometimes in less than a month. Bottom-line is that you always want to be paying attention.

Q: For real estate specifically, what's the best thing to renovate and when's the best time to do it?

A: An important question. Every market might be a little different, but paint is your best friend. Kitchen and baths are often one starting place for many investors and homeowners because of the bang for your buck. But depending on the investment and the goal for the property, these can be done best prior to ultimate sale.

Insider's Tip

Don't get complacent. Stay on top of what interests you in the market. This is what I meant about how your leisure time changes as you grow your wealth: you find yourself naturally wanting to learn more. And those areas you follow are where you'll be most knowledgeable.

CHAPTER 21

MORE PROPERTY, NEW BUSINESSES, AND PLAY

This chapter is solely devoted to highlighting the rewards of your financial freedom. Still, it also helps to highlight how what you love and your work can merge into something completely different and wonderful.

In this chapter, you'll learn about:

- The rewards from all your hard work as it pays off in ways you can only imagine
- Funneling your efforts back in on each other for even bigger benefits
- How your skills from wealth generation carry over to other domains
- The importance of play, as well as your friends and family

B efore we move on, you'd probably like to hear a little bit about what all this financial freedom actually gives you. After all, if you aren't buying all the luxury items you set your eyes on, what can you do to enjoy your wealth generation?

When Jason and I turned 40, we realized that our financial situation had opened up fresh avenues of business, play, and philanthropic endeavors for ourselves.

As you saw in our previous chapters, we were already able to enjoy paying for our friends and family to come to our wedding. And this is only the tip of the iceberg. Over the years, we comfortably lived the lifestyle we desired, not giving up on any of our other passions. So, how did we enjoy our wealth?

As we attained financial freedom, Jason fulfilled his dream of racing a modified race car. As someone who's less familiar with the ins and outs of racing, even I was impressed by the power behind this vehicle. And every time he had to buy a new engine, a somewhat frequent occurrence in the racing world, I bought a well-chosen, stunning piece of jewelry.

We would even start a race shop to build dedicated race cars. How many people can say that they've done that?

But it wasn't all fun and games. We were most grateful to be able to use our money in the following ways at the time.

Unfortunately, Jason's mother, Clarice, passed away during this time period. His parents had worked hard and were proud to be able to leave their five children a small inheritance. Because of our financial security at the time, we happily declined acceptance of Jason's inheritance, giving it to a sibling who didn't have a partner to support her. This enabled his sister to pay off her home and eventually retire.

In addition, another subcontractor who did painting for us was losing the family farm he had inherited. It had been in his family for decades, and it was all he had left. So, we stepped in and purchased the home. He paid us the amount of our payments until a time in the future when he could obtain a loan and buy it back from us.

To recount a few more examples: Another contractor decided to move out of town and had run out of money renovating a home. We paid to re-carpet their home, so they could put it up for sale, and we were repaid at closing.

A couple family members were living on a fixed income and barely getting by. We gave each $300 a month for the rest of their lives. It's amazing how a little money can change someone's life.

But these aren't the only examples we have; there's even more.

For example, a repeat client came into trouble with one of his rental properties. Unfortunately, a police officer was murdered in the alley behind his rental home. At the time, an offer came in low on the duplex, and the client needed $10,000 to close the sale. But his money was tied up in oil stocks, so we stepped in and paid the money to close the sale. He repaid us within 6 months.

An agent on our team approached us, because she had found the property of her dreams, a Frank Lloyd Wright home in Two Rivers, Wisconsin. She had a vision for the home, but no resources to purchase and do the rehab. We bought the home and did extensive rehab. In return, she coordinated the efforts. We made her a partner on a handshake and paid her 25% of the profits when we sold the home a couple years later.

One more example: one day, we met a Russian couple who was losing their home in foreclosure. But they didn't want their handicapped daughter to know. So, we purchased the home and let them rent it back by paying the amount of our mortgage payments on the home on an indefinite lease...

the daughter never found out. Unfortunately, the home would burn down a couple years later, and while they had always kept personal insurance for their belongings, they had let it lapse two months before the fire. They were in their 70s, and they lost everything because they had no insurance. So, we gave them $5,000 to get started in another home.

The best part of being wealthy is being able to share with others and make decisions that can help change someone else's life. We are so thankful for this opportunity.

And that's the real story of financial independence. With our cash flow, we could green light a new business idea from our existing hobbies and interests or step in and help family, friends, or clients. Now, I want to be clear: at no point did we make money off our family or friends. We never charged interest or expected anything back in return.

In no time, we were generating more and more revenue from a few of our business ventures. Did all of them work out in the long run? Of course not. But we could enjoy the fact that our situation allowed us these pursuits for leisure and wealth.

A word on business: as you can imagine, the skills we had developed in our quest for financial freedom carried over fairly easily. Whether you're talking about managing a team or cutting through the numbers to make a final decision, the experiences were incredibly adaptable to our new projects. We had also become exceptionally able to spot bullshit when we saw it, a concern in just about every occupation on the face of the planet.

Still, we also surrounded ourselves by people who mirrored our energy. Mark and John were still with us (and still are with us to this day), but our friends and family had come along for the ride as well. The entire time, all these business enterprises were channeling cash back into our financial freedom. Above all else, we loved what we were doing, and we loved the people who have been by our side through it all. This fact has made all the difference in having wealth for a time but being unhappy versus attaining financial freedom and experiencing the joy of an amazing life.

Frequently Asked Questions

Q: What if I've already run a small business in the past, and I'm not interested in doing so again?
A: That's perfectly okay! When I mentor a new investor, I like to stress how every market is different but so is every person. Our journey to financial freedom means you can do things on your terms. That's the whole point! If you don't want to manage a business, for example, you're free to hire someone else to do it for you if that's your desire.

Q: How will I know when I can start buying my own race cars or fine jewelry?
A: The answer is your cash flow! Just like you don't want to quit your job until you've attained enough cash flow, you also want to wait on big purchases until your situation is right. You don't

have to wait until you've attained $1,000,000 either; in fact, you can start enjoying your own wealth creation far sooner.

Q: With everything you have to do to grow your wealth and run businesses, how do you find time for friends and family?

A: I make time for them. The truth is that, like with anything else, you must ensure that it's a priority. You'll find that when you do so, however, you'll be giving yourself one of the biggest benefits of financial freedom, and that's being with the wonderful people you've chosen to be part of your journey. Though I must admit, one of my goals at all times has been to create additional time to nurture relationships.

Insider's Tip

Before you run out and start any old business, create a list of activities or subjects you appreciate. Although not all of them will make sense for you, several are likely to be starting points for secondary revenue sources and increased cash flow.

CHAPTER 22

WARNING LIGHTS: LOOKING FOR OTHER PLACES

In this chapter, we'll see exactly why you can't let the rewards go to your head. As many readers will remember, the 2008 financial crisis blindsided many, from the investment world to the average home buyer. However, long before it all happened, my team was already seeing the signs and had begun taking action to position ourselves to minimize the potential impact.

In this chapter, you'll learn about:

- The fact that financial freedom is just as much about caution as it is reasonable risks
- When even the experts got it wrong, spectacularly wrong
- The positive side of financial freedom during large cyclical downturns
- Staying rational during downturns and capitalizing on anomalies as you see them

I t was 2001, and I was sitting at my desk, reviewing our monthly numbers. And what I was seeing had me concerned.

Between that year and the previous year, the properties we were looking at had doubled from what we would have paid previously. Even though rents were still there, and our cash flow was solid, there were other worrying aspects to the situation.

For example, many of you will remember in the years leading up to 2008 how just about everyone was trying to buy a house. Think back to what I said about the Fed changing their approach and momentum accelerating, and you can imagine what happened as that trend continued. With almost everyone clamoring to get into a house, the renters that were left over were often the least credit-worthy, among other factors. These conditions made me uncomfortable, as I saw the numbers changing.

On the face of it, all was good in the economy, and everywhere you looked, people were saying the good times would never end. This is as much true whether we're talking about the so-called experts on the financial news or the individuals with no plan or goal who were trying to flip whatever homes they could find. Add in the issue that rents had started to stall, and at this point in our journey, you can probably guess how I was feeling.

Across the country, it seemed like just about everyone was swept up in the home buying craze, and I could sense that much of it was being driven by emotion, not numbers. And my feelings were only confirmed by my cash-on-cash return. And beyond what the pundits are ever saying, you must trust your numbers and your critical thinking. After all, you're the one who knows your market, right?

In our next chapter, we'll look more in-depth on how market cycles work, but for now, be content to know that at this moment in my journey, I was beginning to see the extremes of an expansion phase. During this cycle of the market, you must be notably cautious, as people's optimism gives way to an intense flurry of irrational decisions.

These were the warning lights, and as I sat there in my office reviewing numbers, I could clearly see the signs. When it comes down to it, financial freedom is equally about caution, during certain phases of the market, as it is taking reasonable and calculated risks at other times. However, with wealth creation comes the ability to turn back to your resources and make the decisions that will preserve your financial freedom, instead of getting caught up in the hype.

Of course, my numbers primarily reflected my market, so it got me interested... what was happening elsewhere? Could I diversify myself into less vulnerable markets, and if so, how could this be used to preserve my financial freedom?

I started searching and wondering if every market was like Minneapolis or St. Paul, when I stumbled on a group called RealSource. They sent a questionnaire about our investment goals, and with it and based on their market research, we identified a few places that might meet my goals.

So, we flew out to Biloxi, Mississippi.

As we toured the area, it began to dawn on me that my goal hadn't changed, but what my market was giving me had. And the market in Mississippi? Although the lending practices had been eased across the country, the market in this state was slightly different. What if I could shift my assets around, and if I was correct that a storm was coming, continue to produce cash flow?

In the end, I sold three of my properties in Minnesota and bought three new ones in Mississippi. At the same time, I paired back some of my deals and re-assessed my financial situation. And in the proceeding few years, just like when I started out many years ago, other investors, real estate agents, lenders, and the like thought I was crazy.

That trip changed my investment life. On it, I was taught a concept called Market Timing. You see, I had been a top real estate agent in the area for over 13 years now and never heard of the concept. It was simply not something that was widely taught at the time.

After investing in Biloxi, I applied the same principles to other market places. In turn, we invested in Wisconsin, Montana, Mississippi, and Florida, utilizing Tax-Deferred Exchanges to transfer our wealth to other areas.

A few more years passed. The government had put pressure on the banks, and the banks reacted and lowered their standards. Instead of experiencing a correction as early as 2002, this meddling with our market caused the market to soar. And soar. And soar.

One way I like to explain it is that usually you need to meet three criteria to get a loan. These are:

1. Credit
2. Job
3. Cash

From 2002 until the ultimate crash, you only needed two of the three. Now, imagine if you're unemployed and buy a house. Wouldn't all your friends who were unemployed buy a house? So, they all did for five years! The same goes for cash and bad credit. By the end of the five years, a huge percentage of our population who normally cannot buy a home, bought a home. Only tenants with one of the three above criteria were left to occupy rentals. Not a fun group of tenants.

I remember a trip to Florida in 2004 when I intended on selling my properties. The area real estate agents kept telling me that their market "could only go up, forever." They were wrong! And as a savvy investor, I started making strategic moves. In a few cases, as we neared 2008, I was completely willing to take large cuts in what would be the normal price of business, just to speed up the timeline of a deal. For example, I asked my agent in Montana for the value of our Yellowstone River home. That agent, Jon Ellen, said $1.25M. I told her I wanted it sold in 30 days. She said that it normally takes about a year to sell a home like that. I priced it at $899k and obtained an offer around $850k in 30 days. I asked her later what it would have sold for at the bottom, she said $625k. We still did well as we had purchased for $420k.

My real estate agent in Florida told me I would bring down his whole market if I priced my properties to sell at the price I wanted to sell them. I said, "Unfortunately, you don't see what I see coming. List them now." On one freshwater pool home, we obtained an offer for $599k, but the buyer couldn't close. So, we waited. At the year point, the buyer said they could only pay $549k. I immediately accepted and closed. That home would be eventually worth $140k. We had purchased it new for $249k.

Yet, I knew to trust my own thinking and numbers.

Not long after, I toured some of those same neighborhoods in Minnesota, the ones I had sold homes in. I distinctly recall seeing several houses that I had sold for considerable sums to other investors. What had become of them in only a handful of months? The city was debating tearing them down, because no one was willing to pay for them, not a single penny.

It was a trying time for many people throughout the country, including myself. Though I had made moves to preserve my financial freedom, this period of the market wasn't without its trials. However, my situation could have been far different had I trusted other investors and bankers at the time.

How can you, as someone who values financial freedom, best position yourself in the next economic downturn? For that answer, we turn to a review of market cycles and Market Timing in the next chapter.

Frequently Asked Questions

Q: Is the goal of your financial freedom always cash flow?
A: Yes, and almost always! By retaining that liquidity, you're able to afford yourself the lifestyle you want, from paying your own bills to starting new businesses.

Q: How can diversifying your properties help when the entire economy is crumbling?
A: We'll discuss in a moment how local markets can feed back into larger markets, but for now, think of it like a chain of lakes. A dry spell may come along and sap them of their water, but it's unlikely that all of them will run dry. In the long run, the water has to come somewhere, and you want to go where it is.

Are you concerned about your individual market and how it might impact your wealth? As a successful multi-market investor, I can relate. Let's schedule a conversation to talk about your specific market during an investment coaching session:

http://www.TerryandJason.com/Apply

Q: As a successful investor, what emotions did you experience during the financial crisis?
A: Probably about the same as everyone else. First, I felt vindicated that my assessment was correct when everyone had initially told me it was wrong. Still, lots of people were hurting, and at times, I felt anger, sadness, and much more. Being a successful investor doesn't mean you don't feel emotions; it merely means you put your vision first.

Insider's Tip

I can't stress enough how critical it is to be connecting the dots on your own. Although I do pay attention to the financial news and what other investors are telling me, you can't beat doing the math yourself.

CHAPTER 23

MARKET CYCLES & INVESTING IN OTHER STATES

We're now ready to talk about one of our more advanced financial concepts. In this chapter, we'll see how local and national real estate markets come together historically and the implications for timing your deals.

In this chapter, you'll learn about:

- The natural ebb and flow of every market on the planet
- Working in tandem with market cycles, not necessarily against them
- Diversifying into other states to take advantage of market cycles
- Understanding how multiple markets form the big picture

L et's hit the rewind button just a bit.

In the years leading up to 2008, we had continued to branch out to several different cities. From Montana to Wisconsin to Mississippi and Minnesota to Florida, we were diversifying our assets into markets with different cycles.

But what is a market cycle and how does it apply to your wealth generation?

Historically speaking, every market goes through three revolving periods. This is as much true whether you're talking about any city or metropolitan area. Bottom-line: every market is cyclical; for every up, there is a down. For those of you who lived through the 2008 financial crisis, you'll remember that the euphoria suddenly felt like it dropped off a cliff. This was, at its very core, the rapid transition from an expanding market to a declining marketing.

Although that market period was particularly pronounced, markets across the globe experience more minor versions of these cycles on a regular basis. Not all markets are at the same place in the cycle at the same time. The advantage of understanding these cycles gives you the ability to seek another market when your current market doesn't meet your investment goals.

So, what do these cycles look like?

First, there is the absorption phase. Absorption takes place after the decline part of the cycle. Depending on the depth of the decline, you might find lots of foreclosures and short sales on the market. Lenders are very cautious in the beginning of the absorption process because their recent experience was during the decline. As a result, they're very strict on lending requirements and often increase the down payments and credit score criteria. Very slowly, we begin to sell more properties than the number being listed, which causes a decreasing inventory of property. If this happens consistently over a six-month period, you're definitely in the absorption time period. In addition, it's significant because, as the existing inventory count decreases and we have less than 180-day inventory of homes, the market becomes a seller's market. For great deals, buyers may also compete for homes. Absorption can last a few years or a decade, depending on economic factors. Towards the end of absorption, the lenders start relaxing some of their standards because their recent three-year history of loans likely improved as the decline ended.

Our second market cycle is the expansion phase, which is defined by an acceleration in the decreasing inventory of homes. You'll also find more competitive offers, and interest rates could begin to rise because overall economic activity is better. At the start of this phase, you'll likely get the safest return on your investments when you sell properties you bought from the absorption period. Unemployment is low, the economy is good, and the further we get into the expansion phase, the more frenzied the buying gets. You can't predict when the expansion phase will end. Economic factors can contribute but catastrophic events like 9/11, terrorism, or a stock market crash could turn the market on a dime.

And lastly, the declining market. Those that are paying attention will know we have entered the decline phase as much as 18 months before you see it in the news. Slightly, ever so slightly, a few more homes stay on the market longer. The inventory starts to grow, slowly at first, and suddenly, as the public realizes what is happening. After the public catches on, suddenly, there's a glut of homes for sale. Last time, the banks still gave out loans for 12 months after the decline had started because their recent data showed no trouble in the past. Workers start to lose their jobs as the economy worsens and unemployment rises. The sudden rise of fuel costs hurt the blue-collar workers in our last downturn. At that time, they had to choose between paying for fuel to get to work and put food on the table or pay their mortgage payment. Banks are also tightening their lending standards during this period, and foreclosures are hitting the market. This period, even for local markets, can be quite significant. You'll likely see changes being proposed to anything from interest rates being lowered to stimulate the economy to government incentives to try and delay a downturn. As more homes are listed than the number that are being sold, the market changes into a buyer's market. And different strategies work for investors in a buyer's market. Short sales, foreclosures, and owner financing are in abundance. Still, not every downturn is as significant as experienced by most in 2006-2012. Some are slight and do not affect everyone.

Truthfully, every market, whether it's single-family homes in California or apartment buildings in Cape Cod, go through these three cycles. Without doubt, they usually experience these trends at different periods, but there's a bit more to this investing phenomena. They don't just go through the cycles at differing times; they also may experience them to different degrees or intensities.

An example will help depict what we're talking about: While people may think of the market as a monolithic beast, you know that the devil is in the details, as they say. Think back to 2008. For those of you who might have been too young to remember, this period was filled with market fears. However, if you look closely, you'll see that regions experienced the financial crisis very differently.

Take areas of Florida, for example. Because this state had markets considered to be "hot spots" leading up to the crisis, its decline was far deeper and more pronounced than elsewhere. In some cities, you couldn't drive down the road without seeing endless foreclosures. Still, in the following year, rents shot up an inconceivable amount relative to what they were previously. For investors such as myself who targeted vacation homes in this market, we were in a phenomenal position once the storm was passing.

But let's turn to Montana, where I also owned property. The investors who had focused on this market weren't hurt as badly as ones who say, were holding properties to flip in Florida. And those of us who had balanced our portfolios for optimal cash flow were in a much better position to take advantage of emerging opportunities as the market shifted back into an absorption period.

In reality, the US real estate market is a microcosm of the global financial market, and in turn, it's composed of many smaller markets. You may even be surprised to learn that, in today's hyper-connected world, the economy in one country can affect the real estate purchasing in another, and that's only the start!

But remember, for your journey to financial freedom, we don't want to overcomplicate the picture. You can spend a lifetime trying to fully understand how one factor in a certain area feeds back into another. For now, be confident that market cycles offer you access to unprecedented deals, if you can spot them.

And now that you know about market cycles, you'll see them everywhere.

Frequently Asked Questions

Q: How will I know the best way to balance my portfolio to weather downturns in my market?

A: By knowing your market backwards and forwards! Truthfully, the answer will differ based on your local and national market, but also the depth of their current cycles.

Q: So, what methods should I use to determine whether my portfolio should consist of assets like rental properties, flips, or buy and holds?

A: This is an easier question to answer than our previous one, and that answer is: your cash-on-cash return. In the decline and early absorption phases, flips and wholesaling are easier to find. I love buy-and-holds in the decline and absorption phases. When I'm in expansion, I like to get in and out because I don't know when the top will be.

Q: What tools are available to better understand or visualize market cycles?

A: In my seminars on financial freedom, I provide an outline of market cycles, and it includes a visual aid with a few historical examples. You can grab this resource right from my website, free-of-charge:

http://www.TerryandJason.com/Downloads

Insider's Tip

Study the historic data as much as you stay on top of your market's current trends. Many regions and asset classes go through remarkably similar cycle lengths and depths, and you can glean a wealth of information from what has happened before.

CHAPTER 24

ANALYZING THE RETURNS ON YOUR INVESTMENTS

In this chapter, we break down the methods you'll want to use to understand the returns on your investments. Once you've waded through the numbers, you'll have a better perspective on whether or not a property is worth your time.

In this chapter, you'll learn about:

- How to determine your cash-on-cash return
- Strategies to improve your rate of return
- Calculating your total return on investment
- Positive factors that affect your investments

Nothing can be more key to building wealth with real estate than analyzing the returns on your investment. Once you learn how, it makes it very easy to determine if you should purchase a specific property. At the same time, it also helps you make decisions about whether it's a good idea to renovate the same property. Furthermore, it can be instrumental in helping you make the decision on whether to refinance and get your seed corn out or ultimately sell, whether by an outright sale or utilizing a Tax-Deferred Exchange.

One of the biggest mistakes I see investors make is not re-evaluating their investment on an annual basis. They make the decision to buy a property because it's a good investment and then sit back to enjoy the ride, never realizing that their investment is no longer making the cash-on-cash return of the initial years.

Put simply, cash-on-cash return is the rate of return, and it's often used to calculate the cash income earned on the cash invested in a property. The ratio of annual before-tax cash flow to the amount of cash invested is expressed as a percentage.

What does this look like in practice? A basic example would be:

You purchase a duplex for $200,000 using a 25% down payment of $50,000 and finance the balance. Let's say the total rents for the building are $2,700 monthly, and the monthly expenses are $1,200 PITI (principal, interest, taxes and insurance), plus $75 lawn care. Let's also say your tenants pay utilities.

For this example, the cash flow per month would be $1,425. Is this a sound investment?

We don't know yet. You still need to consider how much of your initial cash outlay you get back in one year. To do so, multiply the monthly cash flow by 12 for annual cash flow and divide by the cash invested. In this case, you put $50,000 down plus $8,000 closing costs. So, divide 17100/58000 and get 29% cash-on-cash return.

Is 29% a solid return on investment?

Yes, probably, but it also depends on your goals. Remember from previously, to become a billionaire, you need to earn a 30% total return on your investment annually and this is 29% cash-on-cash.

The pitfall of most investors is that they don't do the equation in the years following the purchase. Instead, they assume all is good. However, it's my professional investor opinion that you should estimate the value of the property annually.

Let's look at the numbers on this duplex after 5 years when it's valued at $280,000. At this time, it represents the same cash flow per month because it wasn't refinanced. However, the equity position has changed. There is at least $130,000 in equity. So, divide 17100/130000 to get 13% cash-on-cash return.

Hmmm, the cash-on-cash is decreasing with increased equity.

If your goal is to maintain a 30% total return on investment, there are a couple strategies you can take to improve your rate of return:

1. Can your rents increase?
2. Can you refinance, take out some equity, and still maintain a high cash-on-cash return?
3. Can you sell with a Tax-Deferred Exchange and use the equity to buy additional properties to obtain a higher cash-on-cash return?

Now the picture becomes clear.

You might ask, "what is the total return on investment?" There are additional benefits to owning property in addition to cashflow! It just gets better and better!

The IRS treats rental properties favorably. In addition to being able to take all your rental expenses and travel to and from property as a deduction, you get to depreciate the asset minus the land value over 27.5 years currently. Most investors find this depreciation expense off-sets a positive rental cash flow. To figure out the impact of depreciation, multiply by your tax bracket. This amount is the dollar amount on your tax return related to how much the depreciation lowered your taxes.

Another factor has to do with your tenants. Every month when they pay the rent, your principal balance on your loan goes down further. This is called principal reduction, and it's another benefit to owning property.

Appreciation is another positive factor to consider. If you choose a property that is likely to increase in value, appreciation will factor into the equation. Or is there perhaps something you can do to the property to make it worth more money? Do so and increase your total return.

To calculate the total return on investment, simply add:

+Annual Cash flow
+Tax Saving from Depreciation
+Amount of Annual Appreciation
+Amount of Annual Principal Paydown

Divide this number by the Total Cash Invested, or in subsequent years, the Equity, to calculate the total return on investment.

Now if you're not a numbers guru, I may have left you behind. Remember, I used to go to lunch with my calculator before I met Jason. So, don't worry, because I've made a very simple form for you to follow. It isn't fancy, but it will serve the purpose, and you can work through it. Use this link below to download it free-of-charge:

http://www.TerryandJason.com/Downloads

Frequently Asked Questions

Q: Do you always use 30% when it comes to your total return on investment annually?

A: Again, this depends on your specific real estate investment goals, and it can be different, either higher or lower. However, if you find yourself in a more complex situation, pair up with a trusted real estate coach for more expert help.

Q: Would you ever accept a property that didn't meet your criteria and if so, why?

A: In most cases, if it doesn't meet my objectives, I'm not going to accept that property. Now, after decades in the investing world, I've learned that there are plenty of hidden opportunities that others overlook, so I'd certainly run the numbers and consider all the possibilities to make the best decision for my vision.

Q: If I'm not a numbers person, where can I start to get a better grasp on this skill?

A: In my opinion, running the numbers on a property gets easier with time and practice. Today, I can quickly do it all in my head and know in a heartbeat if a property will fit into my goals.

Insider's Tip

When calculating returns on investment, do it the same way every time. You can add possible costs such as a vacancy rate or expenses to repair or rehab. If you do, do so every time so you're comparing apples to apples. In the course of my real estate investing career, Mark, John, Jason, and I would often find multiple properties that we liked. To decide between them, we stopped for lunch, and I pulled out my calculator and figured these numbers. One property rose to the top based on the numbers, making the decision easier.

As mentioned previously, there are apps for your phone that do it for you. I don't recommend using them, not for a new investor. You need to understand the factors affecting your returns and do it yourself. By doing so, you'll be more aware of how to improve your rates in the future. In addition, you don't know what the app maker put into the equation. Something important to them, might not be important to you.

CHAPTER 25

SCORING A PERFECT 10 & CONCLUDING THOUGHTS

Before we wrap up our story, we want to look at one more concept. In this chapter, we'll see what the difference is between being a decent investor versus becoming an expert in the field. Sometimes the distinction can seem minor, but it separates the truly financially free from the rest of the pack.

In this chapter, you'll learn about:

- How subtle attitudes make all the difference
- The way people at the top of their game also value their energy
- The need to develop models and pair with a mentor
- Adding your own creativity and not following the crowd

W hat if I told you that even Olympic Gold Medalists consider your energy to be a defining characteristic of your abilities?

Now, what if I told you your energy determines whether you'll merely be okay at accomplishing your goals, or instead, you'll have your goals feed back into your larger vision?

When asked what splits a 9.9 score from a perfect 10, 1984 Olympian gymnast, Peter Vidmar, had an answer both elegant and insightful. In time his answer would become the motto of individuals seeking to find that edge and attain their most longed-for visions. And you'll recognize it in a heartbeat.

"Risk, Originality, and Virtuosity"

But let's talk a little bit about each of these factors, two of which we've covered throughout our journey.

Your virtuosity, a word often used to describe musicians and artists, is a combination of your skill and talent. But it also goes beyond purely technical precision. With it, an award-winning athlete like Vidmar can "wow" his judges and surprise his audience. Through your virtuosity, or put another way, through your energy, you can recognize market anomalies everyone else has overlooked, and you can encompass these in your plans to achieve what others thought impossible. Before others have even realized that an opportunity in your market exists, you've leveraged it for a vision they couldn't ever have seen.

And that vision is your financial freedom.

Still, risk is part of that picture, but not simply risk taken without consideration of your goals. When Vidmar, as a gymnast, wanted to attain greatness on the world stage, he knew that going from a score of 9 to 10 wouldn't be easy. He also knew, in aiming for what he wanted, there would be setbacks along the way. After all, what if he fell during his performance? Or what if he was off by even a fraction of an inch?

However, through his years of experience and dedication to his craft, he was able to attain one of the highest honors we can bestow on an athlete. His risk met the energy he had built up in his profession, and he was handsomely rewarded for it.

So, where does that leave us when it comes to originality?

Often, when I've met someone who is getting into wealth generation for the first time, they want to rush through everything without focusing on the finer points. As you can see from my journey, it took me 12 years to attain millions; yet, for you, you're now armed with my model in a fraction of the time. You also know how critical the details can be when it comes to growing your wealth.

But our last lesson is that you don't want to be doing what everyone else is doing. That way is not the path to a perfect 10, and it certainly isn't the avenue to financial freedom.

For me, the journey has been filled with challenges, but also blessings. I've also been lucky to have had the chance to surround myself with people who share my desire to do big things. On the one hand, it's meant that I had a chance to rehab a luxurious home by Frank Lloyd Wright and be featured on the Fine Living channel for it. On the other hand, it's also meant that I've been able to help those single mothers way back when on Dale Street in Minnesota. Still, we've also enjoyed doing what we wanted on our terms.

So, the final question is: what will you do with your new-found financial freedom?

Frequently Asked Questions

Q: Why does it matter so much if I score a 9.9 versus a 10?

A: Think back to our chapter on energy; those of us striving for 10s will look to surround ourselves with like-minded individuals, and you definitely want to be in the Perfect 10 Club.

Q: Where did you get your inspiration and motivation to continue on, even during the most difficult times?

A: First, my family, friends, and staff, but also, from figures like Peter Vidmar, who gave their all to make magic happen.

Q: When can I start my journey to financial freedom?

A: Right now!

Insider's Tip

I'm always happy to answer questions or provide advice to any like-minded investor. Now that you're on your own journey to financial freedom, stop by my website and drop me a line!

I am also pleased to announce; Jason and I have begun a National Coaching Business! Many of our clients are from other places and have requested we create a program to meet the needs of investors, potential investors, and real estate agents nationwide, including visiting your marketplace. If you have some interest, please contact me for a personal strategy session. We can evaluate the best strategy to meet your specific goals.

Are you interested in talking with us about your American Dream? Let's discover it together! You can schedule a one-on-one appointment now with Terry at http://www.TerryandJason.com/Apply

Please also like us, follow us, and share with others at our site http://www.TerryandJason.com.

I'd also love to know what you think of the book! Please feel free to review it on Amazon.

Onward!

Together we achieve more!

Hugs,

Terry Records

APPENDIX

SELECT, REAL-LIFE EXAMPLES FROM MINNESOTA & WISCONSIN

Because I've successfully invested in so many properties in various areas of the country, I'm often asked for more detail on many of them. And we love talking about properties! So, here are a few examples of the properties we owned and my thoughts about each one. When you browse them, you'll start to see how to invest differently based on the Market Timing cycle we are in at the time.

230 N. Dale St. Purchased for $5,011 each 11/20/92. These properties were rehabbed and rented; at first at $650 a month and eventually for $1,200. After a full architectural before-selling rehab, they sold on 7/2/2001 for $235,000 through a 1031 Exchange.

232 N. Dale St. Purchased 11/20/92 and same as above but sold for $215,000 through a 1031 Exchange.

1166 Thomas Ave. Purchased for $10,000 in 1994 and sold for $99,900 on 8/9/2000 with a 1031 Exchange.

675 Fuller Ave. Mark and John's first purchase this property on 3/14/96 for $69,300 for the triplex, where later, Jason would rent the top floor when we started dating.

664 Edmund. Purchased on 1/26/98 for $26,200 and is the second property I sold Jason. He made me fill a dumpster here on our first Valentine's Day. He sold it on 4/14/99 for $58,000. And let me tell you, closing day was eventful. We had heard reports that there had been a walk-by shooting the night before and then the other agent called me to say the buyer wasn't getting the loan because of an old judgment for $3k which had appeared on their credit. It took Jason about 15 seconds to agree to pay off the judgment in order to close. We obviously didn't want a walk-by shooting to affect Jason's property.

846 Margaret. This duplex was purchased in 5/15/98 for $59,900 and cash-flowed at about $800 a month. I decided to sell when I thought the market might be nearing a top on 8/28/2004 for $185,000 using a 1031 Exchange. I had also renovated in-between tenants' years before.

358 Maria. Jason purchased this duplex that had 3-bedroom units and only for $62,000 while it would cash flow at $1,000 a month. This helped him reach his goal of quitting his job. The home was sold near the top of the market but just after a person was stabbed on the sidewalk next door.

32 Mounds Blvd. Terry originally purchased this property for just about $50,000 as a foreclosure. It would be renovated and sold to an elderly couple for $129,900. Truthfully, we loved the home and told them we would buy it back in the future if they needed to sell. The husband had health issues, and we did in fact buy it back for $149,900 a short time later. After that, we converted it to a vacation rental until we sold for $201,000 on 3/17/2005 in a 1031 Exchange. It was called "Sacred Ground," because it faced the bluff overlooking the city of St. Paul on Dayton's Bluff. We had many great memories there, where our foreman for one of our crews, who also worked on our properties was married by a longtime staff member, Holli Taff, in 2003.

1408 Edgerton. This duplex was purchased on 9/22/99 for $106,500. We had noticed the prices were up, but we still purchased it, because it made sense for our goals. At the time, we were buying for cash flow and the rents had risen enough to support the increased prices. Of course, everyone remembers what they're doing that day, 9-11-01, right? We were renovating this property at the time, and our tenant had left and had also left us thousands of cockroaches. After spending 15 seconds in the home that day, I remember feeling like they were crawling all over me. We re-rented at the time and sold on 2/09/2005 for $194,900 with a 1031 Exchange.

1488 Sherburne. This property was purchased on 12/8/99 for in$131,000. Honestly, it had a nice floor plan, and we would eventually sell it on 7/6/04 for $220,700 using a 1031 Exchange.

1483 Grand Avenue. Property was purchased on 1/20/2002 for $193,000. Jason added architectural detailing, and we re-sold on 1/15/2003. We knew the market wasn't going to last so we opted to get out ASAP.

880 Wilson Ave was a large, 4-unit building on the Eastside. There were 17 bids on the home, and we bid $33k over asking to purchase the opportunity for $177,000 on 2/18/2002. Because of the number of bedrooms, it would bring in a solid $2,000 cash flow per month after renovations were complete. Of course, Jason renovated by installing new kitchens and baths. And the building was beautiful when he was done. I got to thinking about it and on a hunch, I put it up for sale and obtained $450,000 on 9/7/2002. Awesome!

617 Ottawa. This is the duplex we previewed on that memorable Super Bowl Sunday. We bought it on 1/31/01 for $173,900 and sold 5/28/2003 for $247,900, not wanting to wait for the bubble to burst and completed a 1031 Exchange, so we could move money to Florida.

32 Dunlap Ave South. We purchased this one as an office space for our team on 10/15/2001, soon after 9/11/01. It's in a trendy area of St. Paul, and we were able to convert it to commercial space.

Jason also added a handicap bathroom and wheelchair lift. However, we were worried about the imminent crisis, so we sold on 10/5/2006, giving the buyer a second mortgage with owner financing. Even though no one else knew yet, I knew the crisis was coming. When this buyer soon

defaulted on the second mortgage we had given her, we did not pursue it. She had lost everything, and we did not want the property back as it would have been worth less than what she had paid us originally and owed.

976 Robert St #102 was bought during the downturn for $26,000 on 6/27/2007. We would rent this one and eventually re-sold it for $55,750 on 4/1/8/13.

The Bernard Schwartz House, a Frank Lloyd Wright Usonian home in Two Rivers Wisconsin was purchased with 1031 Exchange money. This was the dream home of one of our agents, Lisa Proechel. She desperately wanted to buy this home and turn it into a vacation rental and asked us to step in. Together, we lovingly restored the home, and we were honored when it was featured on the Fine Living Channel. We sold it to one of Lisa's friends just before the bust for a tidy profit. It's still a lovely vacation home today.

In summary, most of our original purchases were bought strictly for cash flow per month. After building a large portfolio and seeing our starting money become at-risk for a potential downturn, we moved our money to other states to find new opportunities to invest with another point in the market cycle. We also expanded the types of properties we invested in. At one point, we owned 12 vacation rentals in different states, two real estate office buildings, and a race shop, in addition to our regular rentals. If you start with the basics of investing, you can use your original investments as foundation blocks to help you achieve your ultimate dream.